# THE INCREDIBLE JOURNEY

BY
REVEREND
CAROL RUTH KNOX, PH.D.

COY F. CROSS II, PH.D.
EDITOR

Koho Pono, LLC

**The Incredible Journey**

Published by Koho Pono, LLC
Clackamas, Oregon USA; http://KohoPono.com

The right to publish the works of Carol Ruth Knox is licensed by Coy F. Cross II through an agreement with Unity of Walnut Creek. All of Carol Ruth Knox's work is owned and copyrighted by Unity of Walnut Creek.

Second Paperback Edition 15august2014

ISBN: 978-1-938282-12-6 (trade paper)
ISBN: 978-1-938282-13-3 (eBook)


Manufactured in the United States of America

"This book offers depth and perspective for those who are choosing to look below the surface for insights that resonate with their soul. I appreciate how Carol Knox's experiences take the reader inside her world as she offers the gems of her life's work."

*- Gail Derin, Licensed Unity Teacher*

" 'The Incredible Journey' describes the spiritual 'unfoldment' of the Reverend Carol Ruth Knox, one of Unity's most dynamic ministers. She inspired a generation of congregants and young ministers, including me, to search deep within themselves for that Divine connection which has the answers to our most profound questions. I recommend Carol Ruth's 'Incredible Journey' to anyone seeking guidance and support for their own spiritual exploration."

*- Rev Beth Ann Suggs, PCC; Unity Minister*

"I loved Carol's teachings... I was immediately drawn to them from the first time that I heard and read them. She was the beginning of my knowing that I also was a mystic."

*- Dr. Marj Britt, Senior Minister, Unity of Tustin*

"Carol Ruth Knox was responsible for my becoming a Unity minister. I had lost the ritual of going to church and was in my own 'wilderness' experience. A friend called me the morning Carol Ruth was killed and I ran to church and virtually never left...."

*- Cindy Bruce, Unity Minister*

"Carol Ruth Knox will take you from the mundane to the metaphysical as you read her words. She was a spiritually gifted teacher who used her own growth as stepping stones to teach the path of God. She was a mentor and great friend whose love of life was shared by all. I loved her deeply."

*- Jo Coudray, Member, Unity of Walnut Creek*

"As a Unity Minister of 27 years and a psychotherapist of 35, I have met 100s of teachers whose teachings have influenced me. However, only a few remain in an inner circle of influence and they are always with me and guiding me along the way: Rev. Carol Ruth Knox is one of these people."

*- Rev. Suzanne Carter, M.A., L.P.C., Unity Minister*

# DEDICATION

*I dedicate this book to Carol Ruth Knox, my mentor and my friend, and to Carol Martha Cross, my beloved and muse.*

# TABLE OF CONTENTS

# FOREWORD BY COY F. CROSS II, PhD

When I met Reverend Carol Ruth Knox in October 1980, I knew my life was about to change forever. Over the next six years, she became my teacher, my mentor, my minister and my dear friend. I came to rely on her wisdom, her insight, her compassion and her friendship as I navigated an especially difficult period of my life.

On February 1, 1987, all that changed when an intruder killed Carol Ruth. Like many others, I was overwhelmed by disbelief, anger, pain and sadness. We had come to depend on her Sunday talks, classes and counseling to guide us through life's challenges. Where could we turn now? As I pondered this question, I remembered her basic message, "You cannot depend on my always being there. Your answers lie within."

Soon after Carol Ruth's transition, I committed to ensuring her teachings - lessons that had changed my life - would not be lost. Like many important undertakings, this one has not followed a straight line.

I spent several years gathering material from various sources. Then I had difficulty finding time to write about Carol Ruth. I was working as an Air Force historian and my mind couldn't make the leap from writing about military operations during the day and profound spiritual Truths at night.

Finally, in March 2007 I retired and began devoting much of my time to Carol Ruth's teaching. I inundated myself in her writings and audio-tapes of her talks. Two years into the project, my wife, also named Carol, was diagnosed with ovarian cancer. I soon shifted my writing's focus to applying Carol Ruth's teachings to being with my wife during her illness. The resultant book is *"The Dhance"*.[1]

In 2013 Unity of Walnut Creek, where Carol Ruth served as minister for 17 years, graciously granted me license for all her material. Later in that year, I edited and published *"The Path of God"*[2], a

---

[1] Coy F. Cross II, *The Dhance: A Caregiver's Search for Meaning* (Clackamas OR: Koho Pono, LLC, 2012).

[2] Carol Ruth Knox, ed. Coy F. Cross II, *The Path of God* (Clackamas OR: Koho Pono, LLC, 2013).

compilation of eleven Sunday lessons Reverend Knox gave in 1986.

Working with Carol Ruth's lessons has brought me unexpected gifts. First, I felt a great loss in 1987 when my friend made her transition, not only the loss of her person, but also the loss of her wisdom. In editing material for the first book, I realized her teachings were still available to me. I also discovered videos of Sunday talks I didn't know existed, so I can experience a sense of her presence that I have been missing.

My second gift, I have reconnected with innumerable others who share my love of Carol Ruth's message. Some people I have known previously, others are new friends. Several have expressed their gratitude that the teachings are being preserved and made available.

My last gift has been introducing new people to Carol Ruth through Sunday talks, workshops and classes. Twenty-seven years after her transition, her message is still relevant and capable of moving people to tears, to action, and to change.

This book, *"The Incredible Journey"* is Carol Ruth's autobiographical account of her personal unfoldment and her map to aid other spiritual seekers on their path. I am honored and privileged to be the vehicle to bring this modern mystic's story to a larger audience.

I am grateful to: Reverend David McArthur, Senior Minister at Unity of Walnut Creek, and the Center's Board of Directors for granting me the license for this material. I'd like to thank "The Carol Ruth Knox Foundation" for its efforts to preserve Carol Ruth's teachings and initially publishing *"The Incredible Journey"*. I'm also grateful to Scott Burr and Dayna Hubenthal of Koho Pono Press for their professional help and constant advice and support; my friend Gail Derin for her expert eye in editing, my family for their continued love and support; and especially to my late wife Carol for her encouragement and unfailing belief in me.

*Carol Ruth Knox speaking at Unity of Walnut Creek
(Coy and Carol Martha Cross are in the lower left corner)*

# REV.CAROL RUTH KNOX'S INTRODUCTION

This is not the beginning of your Incredible Journey. You have been on this path for a long time and have turned to these pages as yet another step in a life-long process that has been pushing, working and expanding you. Perhaps it is your desire to be more fully aware of this process that has led you here. Perhaps it is a more immediate issue, a life crisis that compels you.

Life continually grows us. We are never finished. The force, the energy responsible for our growth is "life's need to become". It is a creative process, an ever-evolving movement toward oneness with our God self. Like the seed growing to full flower, reseeding and growing again, this energy continues to expand us into progressively deeper levels of consciousness.

We humans have many ways of coping with this energy in us, many alternate routes on our journey. Some people, guided by their minds, travel via philosophy, some via mind-altering substances. Others cope by relying upon emotional instincts. Some develop their physical prowess, while others attempt to purge physical sensation through esoteric disciplines. Many turn to therapy, many others to religion.

These alternate approaches — intellectual, emotional, psychological, symbolic — all work temporarily. But people too often complain that although certain ways of coping or certain disciplines work for a while, none ultimately leads them to completion. Unsatisfied, and disillusioned, they must resume their journey in search of yet another route.

Spiritual interpretation might well be the last "way of coping" to which we humans resort. We do not "end up" in psychology, for instance; even that becomes limiting and fails to satisfy. We inevitably move on to something else and that something else, finally, is the spiritual. For some it is a chosen path. Many, however, respond to an inner motivation they neither understand nor want.

Jacob Needleman, in his book *"Lost Christianity"*[3],

---

[3] Jacob Needleman, *Lost Christianity* (Garden City NY: Doubleday and Co., 1980).

says that we must realize that spirituality's function, [as are all functions of Life energy], is to expand consciousness, and consciousness expands as we are able to assist in the inner struggle. He writes, "The great church fathers, the great saints, recognized that a specific inner struggle was the foundation upon which metaphysical concepts would guide the transformation of human nature. Intellectual explanation, as such, could lead a person to begin the struggle, but could never and must never take the place of the struggle within."[4]

Our part in participating in this inner struggle is first to recognize that the journey is one of expanding consciousness. Then we must assist in letting the natural stripping away of old conditionings occur and dare to be pushed into the unknown so that Life energy can express through us as our God nature.

This book can guide your participation in that inner struggle and help in your growth and expansion. The material, here, evolved from two previous works, one dealing with the issue of change and the other with the Spiritual Path itself. The more the two were examined, the stronger

---

[4] Ibid., p. 37.

seemed their relationship. They both discuss the mental, emotional, and physical expressions of human experience. They both represent successive stages of the spiritual journey. They also share a common goal: to study the refinement and transformation of human nature in order that more Life energy can express.

In beginning with the material on crisis and change in the first two chapters, we can explore the states in which many people find themselves as a result of something other than their own choice — states often experienced prior to embarking upon the Spiritual Path.

This material is divided into six chapters that serve as signposts or markers on the Incredible Journey. Familiarity with these markers, an understanding of the growth process, may help you chart your own course with new perspective. It is hoped that you will also learn to be more compassionate and patient with yourself along the way.

Chapter 1 presents a scenario of personal crisis that serves as the model for a discussion of the experience. A description and guidelines for addressing physical, mental and emotional symptoms of change in Chapter 2 may aid the reader to shortcut some of the more traumatic parts of the growth process.

The material in Chapter 3, "Understanding Spiritual Growth," is particularly important as it explains aspiration toward God. This is a key motivation for spiritual searching and evolution. The complex catalysts for life changes are also discussed in this section, as are the qualities necessary for participation in one's own spiritual development.

After the overview provided in Chapter 3, the reader is prepared to examine the actual stages of the Spiritual Path in Chapter 4. These include "not conscious" and "conscious" phases, "The Dark Night of the Soul" experience, and conclude with "Beingness" and the integration of Life energy.

Active involvement in the spiritual process is summarized in Chapter 5 and the reader is given powerful tools for developing and refining consciousness.

The final chapter, "Living/Doing the Spiritual Life," deals with the individual's relationship with Self, Earth, other human beings, work and death. Embracing all previous material, this chapter attempts to guide the spiritual being into a sense of harmony and oneness with all of creation, while functioning in the world.

As you proceed upon this Incredible Journey, it may be useful to read the "Question/Answer" section that follows Chapter 6. These have been selected from many asked at seminars on "Change and the Spiritual Path". They can both clarify chapter information and cover related, although divergent, material.

This book is for those people who hunger to be involved in their own spiritual process, who long to take responsibility for their own inner lives. It is also for those caught up in the spiritual movement who are feeling desperate and perplexed. Its content will richly serve those who feel stuck in positive thinking and manipulative religious systems which have worn thin — it provides depth and direction. It is for all who wish to contact the spiritual force that drives them and will not let them find contentment in the external trappings of life. It is a challenging, exciting, re-vitalizing process, truly an Incredible Journey. Enjoy it!

*Reverend Carol Ruth Knox*

*Carol's Beautiful Smile*

*Carol Ruth Knox (right) and her Mom, Gladys, (left)*

# 1: THE EXPERIENCE AND SYMPTOMS

## *A PERSONAL EXPERIENCE*

Few people understand the issue of change. Fewer still have the ability to recognize the enormous potential for growth in the major and minor crises that function as the catalysts for life's changes. People simply do not expect or understand crisis — why should we? We are conditioned to believe that if we place our feet on the well-worn steps and expend sufficient energy to climb them, we can attain the top, the "pinnacle" of success, power, wealth, happiness, love, even contentment. No one expects a different outcome from the one in which they've invested; no one expects to lose control, to fall, to be "leveled" by life.

It certainly wasn't part of my expectations to "fall off the top" of my neat, successful world and be plunged into confusion and despair. As much as I had counseled in crises situations, they had never touched me personally. Maybe I had unconsciously hoped that being a minister would give me safe passage. I'm glad now that it didn't.

A crisis experience alters one entirely. The new dimensions that have been added, the wisdom that in-fills most moments, the feeling of solidarity that strengthens my sense of self and life, could not have come had it not been for this experience. It has taught me that God, the all-pervading sustenance of the universe, is totally in charge.

As an introduction to this issue of change, I will share with you an account of a personal crisis that altered the course of my life in every conceivable way. Perhaps, in reading my experience, you will recognize your own symptoms of change more clearly. Hopefully, you will be more comfortable knowing that you, too, can survive such a crisis and learn new ways of growing and caring for yourself in the process.

My experience started on a Monday afternoon in September 1976. I was sitting in the back yard of my home. My world was a proven success; I was making between $22,000-$25,000 a year; I had just fallen in love eight months prior; I had just returned from a beautiful vacation, my parents were alive and well, my family life was pleasant and abundant; I had completed all of the work for my doctorate with the exception of the dissertation; my body was absolutely healthy as far as I knew. I was at the top, and every goal I had ever set in my life was completed. At that moment, I sat contemplating, staring out into space with the lovely capacity I then had to sit and float and adore the Universe I was a part of.

Earlier that day I had seen two counselees who had shared with me tremendous anxiety and depression — one a 43-year-old man who had had a heart attack and had not been able to come back from it; another, a 40-year-old man who shared with me a year of anxiety and the pressures in his home life. I came home to rest, as I always did then from noon to 3:00 PM. As I sat, I absolutely fell off a cliff, and I fell off it inside. The experience was one of feeling like somebody had pulled the rug out from underneath me. It was a physical experience; it felt like an experience I had had once, while trying marijuana, where I totally lost all control. I could not grab hold of my mind. My whole system plunged into "no-where."

When it happened, I had no idea what was going on. All I could do was use everything I knew that was in Unity philosophy at the core of my existence. So I started using affirmations to try to reconnect with reality. I went to the piano and tried to play and could not. I was terribly frightened. When my roommate came home, I told her what had happened, I had no idea what was going on and she could see how frightened I was. By that time I could feel myself coming back 'to life'. That evening I taught a class and broke down. Afterwards I talked with two friends and plunged two more times into the same space. When I awoke the following morning, I felt relatively 'normal'. That sense of normality lasted about a week.

The following Tuesday evening, at dinner, it happened again. For the next year, I proceeded to have these 'attacks' hit me about once every other day. They were never as bad as the original one. Without realizing it, I had moved into a state of extreme anxiety. I lost my capacity to focus and concentrate. I became fearful about going into the world. I became afraid of going into society I would sit at meals and find the energy disappear from me instantaneously. The experience was frightening. I even found I couldn't talk at times — I had nothing to say.

One of the most difficult parts of the experience was that I was still running a Unity Center, and I became fearful about my job, that I might not be able to keep it up. I began waking mornings without the desire to get out of bed. I didn't want to go to work, didn't want to associate with people, and surely didn't know what I was supposed to do with myself. I cried once a week whether I wanted to or not. Whenever I went to the ocean or a beautiful outdoor place, to which I had always related, I would break into tears that would knock me out for the whole day. Once the tears had knocked me out, my mind would come back and start working me, and the worrying process would set in and the fear.

I became fearful that I would lose my love relationship, and I did. I was in the most needing position I have ever experienced in my life, and the relationship was not stabilized enough to serve both of us. I lost the desire to eat. I lost weight. I would go to give a speech, and just before I was to give the speech, have the same experience happen, and wonder how I could ever get through the speech. I asked everybody what was going on with me, what was the cause. I spent nearly all day, every day, looking for a reason and worrying. Few days were happy; I was totally dissatisfied.

My menstrual periods shifted and became much more painful. My body shape changed. There was no peace for me. In June that year, a very good friend suggested that I leave my work and go "get well". I had a Center that supported me through a three-month sabbatical. I did the absolutely wrong thing — I went to the Cape in Massachusetts with my family, where you can't do the kind of work one has to do in this space.

I spent most of the time there worrying and crying. I bought a book on hypoglycemia. I tried a new diet for a day, which was a mistake, because I did have hypoglycemia, but since the results weren't immediate, I stopped. I then went to Hawaii, an island in the middle of the Pacific for five weeks. One should never do that at such a time, never put one's self in the middle of nowhere; one should be near home, with good support systems, but under no pressure.

However, in Hawaii I stopped the worrying and anxiety. I had enough Truth tools to know that I had to get off my own case. At times I considered killing myself. I did find that every time I went down, my down was higher than the previous low, which meant that my desire to end my life stopped appearing about April 1977.

While I was in Hawaii, I was able to do some personal work. I had been taking notes and keeping a journal on all the symptoms during this time; and, with the exception of turning around my thoughts of self-deprecation and despair, I had made little progress. I had little interest in life; but, I started feeling better just by being in nature.

Also, life had lost all its meaning. I confronted that in May and accepted that it was all right for life to have no meaning. I gave up the fight. I started reading Joel Goldsmith. Remember, I am a Unity minister; I had all the spiritual tools to work with, but what happened was that my belief system was not strong enough to survive this kind of attack. So my whole belief system and philosophy went through a total change. While reading Joel Goldsmith's *"Meditation"*[5] one afternoon, I followed the recommendation to go to a Bible passage and read something that caught my mind and meditate upon it. I picked up the phrase in Ezekiel 37:5, "Behold, I will cause breath to enter into you, and ye shall live." I lay on the couch and went very deep inside, farther than I had been able to get for some time since meditation and affirmations had become worn out. As I rested inside, I had a wonderful sense, "Yes, something did breathe life into me." I began to feel life move. One could say that was the seed of the New Birth happening, metaphysically.

I stayed with that idea for about a half hour and went out to take a three-hour walk. I spent that

---

[5] Joel S. Goldsmith, *The Art of Meditation* (New York: Harper Collins Publishers, 1956)

entire walk listening to Carol Knox's inner thoughts, and I found out what a mess they had become. They were full of anxiety, fear and doubt. This time, when they appeared, I simply recognized them and acknowledged them. I had no answers; I realized I was stuck. I began working every day on being aware of these thoughts and related beliefs.

When I felt myself loaded with nervous anxiety, I also read Mary Baker Eddy's *"Science and Health With A Key to the Scriptures"*[6]. Reading, "There are no nerves in Spirit and no Spirit in nerves," helped. In other words, "Spirit doesn't even know that you have a nerve in your body." And I had to learn that, because my body was really shaking. There is no Spirit in nerves either, since Spirit's consciousness has no form. It is absolute purity. That stayed with me and was something on which to cling.

I said that I feared I would lose love; I would lose my job; I would lose everything. Only one of those fears came true. I lost my love.

---

[6] Mary Baker Eddy, *Science and Health With a Key to the Scriptures*. This book was first published in 1875 (publisher unknown; it may have been published by Mary Baker Eddy).

However, when I returned from Hawaii, I came back to a really difficult situation at work. It had not been taken away from me, but it had totally changed in terms of responsibility. I was no longer the head "honcho" at Unity. I was one of a five-member team, part of a New Age organization. My responsibilities were reduced, especially in my own mind, and it seemed obvious to me that those who had created the Center's new organization were seeking to remove me from a position of significant power. I changed my office, moved into a small one, and went back to work. I spent the next eight months wondering what I was supposed to do, which is a very trying situation for a person who is still scared. You see, if you can get lost in your work, you are saved for some part of the day, but I could not.

By way of explanation, this change in responsibility was all done with my agreement, and in love and creativity, by those who had designed this new Center operation. Gradually, I realized it was a blessing, because it gave me more time to fully enter the new me being born.

In September 1977, I went to my dissertation advisor for my PhD, told her what was happening to me, and started working on my dissertation. She suggested I might find my answer in working on the dissertation. The material that I had to read was on the mystical life, which was the direction toward which I was groping. One of the recommended books was called *"The Way of a Pilgrim"*[7], edited by R.M. French. It tells of a pilgrim from Russia who learns to practice the Jesus Prayer: "Lord Jesus Christ, have mercy upon me." Now the words of that prayer are not important, the idea is. He went to a priest, learned to practice this prayer, and after a week, went back to the priest and related that the worst monsters within him had come to the surface. The priest explained that this was natural, that he should continue to be aware, and to keep practicing. Then he advised that the pilgrim say the prayer 3,000 times a day. A week later he increased to 6,000 times a day, then to 18,000, and finally to 36,000 daily. The pilgrim developed sores on his tongue and his inner lips. However, he "got it," and spent the rest of his life traveling about, practicing that inner prayer of the heart and devoting his life to God.

I started doing this work in September 1977, but I started doing it the "Joel Goldsmith way" by

---

[7] R.M. French, trans, *The Way of the Pilgrim and The Pilgrim Continues* (San Francisco: Harper, 1965)

simply sitting inside myself and hearing the words, "I AM." Just before I returned from my sabbatical to the Sunday ministry in September 1977, I drove to Los Angeles holding this prayer in my heart the whole way and watching my thoughts. I then spent the week there practicing this prayer, and returned practicing it, and had a great deal of peace. I had hoped the prayer would be magical and it helped, but I continued having troubles.

Back at work, I was confused about my new duties. I could never get my energy to maintain itself for a full day. I wondered what had happened to good old Carol Knox and longed to recover the wonder-child, the star, the delightful, excited, eager, dynamic, powerful person. That is who I had known me to be. But instead of getting the old Carol, I was finding a wholly new me.

In December 1977, I read St. John of the Cross's "*Dark Night of the Soul*"[8] and for the first time in a year and three months, I found myself in a book. The words were: "In the dark night of the soul you will experience no imagining, no meditations,

---

[8] Saint John of the Cross of the Order of Mount Carmel, *Dark Night of the Soul* (Trowbridge, Wiltshire GB: Redwood Press Limited, 1973)

no fantasies, no dreams." That's exactly how I had been. I could not, in my mind, create fantasies, dreams, imaging, hopes; all I had experienced was desperation. St. John of the Cross gave me a great solace, because he identified clearly that what was happening in me. What I was experiencing had the possibility of being something other than insanity or illness — it could be spiritual, a part of a personal process, a step toward mystical unification!

The month of December 1977 was one of the most mystical months of my life. It was the most high, inspired month, and yet it was also the lowest, because now it had been nearly a year and a half and I was wondering, "Is this thing ever going to end; am I going to have to live this way for the rest of my life?"

The week before the New Year, I went out to dinner three times and became aware that I had eaten candy and wine. Every time I had, I experienced the same symptoms as those in September of 1976. The most significant one was when I went to Los Angeles to be with a friend. I had three pieces of butterscotch candy, a very small glass of wine, was sitting delightfully enjoying the people I was with, and "disappeared inside," even though I had spent the whole day in a high state of pure consciousness, practicing "no-mind". On New Year's Day, I had the same experience again. I knew that something had to be out of whack physically, so I picked up the hypoglycemic diet book by Pavlo Airola[9], read the symptoms, and started the diet immediately. Within two days, my head, my sight, my body, were absolutely different. Stress helped cause and perpetuate the disease. Once I changed my diet, my body became better and the stress lessened.

During the months of January through May 1978, I was committed to getting well. The physical healing that was taking place gave my life focus and helped me to measure my progress. By May I

---

[9] Pavlo Airola, *Hypoglycemia: A Better Approach* (Publisher unknown, 1977)

was beginning to feel a sense of my own power again and moved back into my larger office.

Back in February, I had started creating some goals for myself, like teaching at Unity Village, giving more talks in public, writing a book. The effort that I initiated then, when it looked as if I really didn't have much going for me, flourished by June. This is an important point: sowing one's seeds even though it does not look as if one will be able to gather them up once they are sown.

I did a lot of research on the state of the human mind during this time: what gets people down, why we get depressed, why we hurt, what we are doing to ourselves, what we can do for ourselves. As a result of this research, I realized that I had let my own mind "stagnate" and entertain a great deal of negativity. In the old style and former modes, I had exhausted my creativity. Obviously, new ideas and patterns would have to come from new ways of being. This realization was a powerful stimulus to my healing process.

Another part of my healing had begun as early as 1977. By using effective tools, I began at that time to come out of the depths of my despair. I was again capable of making decisions for progress in my personal life. More significantly, I began to see that what I had experienced were the initial symptoms of a process that would lead to profound spiritual growth and transformation.

In bringing this personal sharing to a close, I will review what I think were the causes for what happened to me. First and most important, I had entered an entirely new level of consciousness, one I could neither handle nor accept. Stress factors — the breakneck pace of my life and the emotional upheaval of a love affair — helped bring on the hypoglycemia which became a compelling catalyst for change. The broad spectrum of my symptoms prompted a many-faceted response and the resulting confusion led to despair. I was required to sort it all out, to understand and learn or give up in insanity or death. I was forced to have to "clean up" many areas of my life in order to dwell in new possibilities.

That is my story. The experience has been physical, mental and emotional. I went into it courageously and let myself think every despairing thought. Through it all, I kept trusting and learning as new possibilities unfolded for me. I have continued to grow closer to God, and the intention for my life has clarified — to be one with Spirit. I am quieter. My emotions have made peace with life. My philosophy has totally changed. My personality has balanced out. I feel cleaner, healthier, more whole. I now have a clearer concept of who I am and who I am becoming; I have changed, and I have learned to accept change as essential to my growth, perhaps even to life itself.

*Reverend Carol Ruth Knox (1986)*

## 2: PREPARING THE BODY TEMPLE

Before beginning, it would be good for you to bring to mind again what you are attempting to accomplish by being involved in this spiritual pursuit. As you read, you may find yourself raising questions and doubting some of the techniques that I have used, so it will be important for you to be sure of your intent.

Realize that your intent is fully within yourself and must be the core around which you are willing to be active, to participate, and to make your value decisions.

A Robert Browning[10] poem states that we are trying to tap the inner splendor, to release it so that it can come forward. The inner splendor is there; the spiritual force is there. That internal potential has never gone anywhere. It has not

---

[10] Robert Browning, "Paracelsus", "... to know rather consists in opening a way out whence the imprisioned splendour may escape."

been blotted out or even covered. It is there to be tapped and released through your participation. We are attempting to attain a state where we can feel unified, where we can feel at peace and in harmony regardless of the circumstances.

Now we have to deal with the question of why we are not in that state all the time. We understand that there are certain situations in our lives that can throw us off center. We understand that we can feel empty and lonely. We understand that our personalities can upset us. Does that mean that we have clouded over this potential or conditioned it out of ourselves? Have we, possibly, even harmed ourselves? The answer is both "yes" and "no".

Obviously, something is not clear, there is some knowledge not revealed, some way in which we are denying ourselves. Not having that clarity, lacking that knowledge, experiencing that denial is not a fault, a flaw or a sin.

You see, the hidden splendor is within and available; the energy source is there to be tapped. At the same time, we have attitudes, beliefs, mesmerisms and actions that shroud it. That is not an error on our part. There is nothing to feel guilty about. There is no sin here. If we accept that something is shrouding it (and I would rather use the word shroud than block, cover, harm, or damage), then our role is to free ourselves from whatever is shrouding us from that ever-present flow.

That is the first activity of participation — to free ourselves from what is blocking us from that flow. The mystery of this is in the process of finding the way of removing the shroud, clearing the web, breaking through the gauze.

To do this, we have to look at the obvious areas where we shroud ourselves: physically, mentally, emotionally and in our lifestyles.

Each person has an individual journey to discover the ways in which they keep themselves from feeling connected. It is a very private journey.

It is as if there are many spokes from the hub to the outside of the wheel. When anybody touches the outside or inside of the wheel, they know that they have touched it. We seek this experience in many different ways, and there is a great deal of confusion. Different people will stress Bhakti Yoga, Raja Yoga, regular Yoga or "born again" experiences. What they are saying is that this is the way they were able to break the covering, to tear through the shroud, to become free.

## AREAS OF PARTICIPATION

### PHYSICAL

One of the greatest areas that I have had to struggle with has been the physical. I didn't fully appreciate, until a few years ago, that the mind, body and emotions are all interconnected. I had lived under a belief that, as long as one is connected with God, then he/she can do anything they want with the rest of themselves. It was a tremendous jolt to me to find out that I couldn't plug into all the energy that I wanted to in the physical realm, in an ongoing way as my teaching and belief system said that I could.

In a group this morning, someone said, "It was such a shock to me the first day that I went to push the button for restoration." What I had to realize was that the proper treatment of my body was a way to connect with God, and that realization comes from an entirely different concept than "eat right, don't smoke, don't drink, don't get too tired," which is a moral concept without an inner realization of why.

In order to connect with the Spirit Within, it is essential that the body become whole and that it be treated well. You cannot be harming your body and expect to attain a feeling of unification and oneness. The body has to be given proper foods.

One evening recently, for example, I was so tired that I thought I should have steak, and I was told I ought to eat something light. It was good advice. The light food served me. I tend to want to eat more and more light food. I have stopped drinking alcohol entirely. I have stopped eating sugar. I have stopped eating meat. I have become acutely aware of the necessity of rest.

In Joel Goldsmith's book *"Awakening Mystical Consciousness"*[11], he states that it is most damaging for spiritual healers or leaders to not take enough time away to protect and care for themselves. He continues: it takes six hours to properly restore yourself, six hours of being alone beyond resting, beyond sleeping at night. We hear accounts of people under stress and strain and the demands they make upon themselves. None of us can expect this connection with Spirit to happen if we are worn out.

I keep coming back to the fact that we are an

---

[11] Joel S. Goldsmith, ed. Lorraine Sinkler, *Awakening Mystical Consciousness* (San Francisco: Harper And Row, 1980).

energy system. And as an energy system we have a limited supply available to us. If you want energy to dedicate to your spirit, to feel this connection and this free-flowing movement, you cannot be dissipating it in lesser important areas of life. You just cannot do it; I don't care how spiritual you are.

## *MENTAL*

The second area from which we have to free ourselves is the mental. The only way to do this is to detach from the mind so it can be free to function as it is intended. Freeing the mind requires a growing being, a profound philosophy, and good skills to assist the process. You will, no doubt, experience fear as you let go of the significance and power of the mind; and that is all a part of the natural process — freedom comes with fear and fear with freedom.

You can learn from feelings; not only by my telling you what they are and why they come, but because they bring life realizations. As they are transformed, they show us about our attachments to life and our conditioned responses. This leads to greater and greater detachment. We become aware of life's illusions and games. Such detachment takes time to accept, but frees us from the agonies we bring to ourselves.

With more learning we see an "Inner Center" begin to take us over. Less and less do we have to consciously "control" our reaction to life and more and more does this Center do the awareness work for us until IT becomes the light and is our Being.

Mystically, the approach to the emotions is that we are Spiritual Beings and nothing else — all the rest is illusion. Therefore, the mystic would say, "There are no emotions in Spirit. There is no mind in Spirit; there are no thoughts in Spirit." Mystics state that the world is primarily illusion, which means that the world does not have an existence separate from Spirit. Using this attitude towards emotions can also be effective.

### *EMOTIONAL*

The third area from which we must free ourselves is the emotional. (Remember, none of these are bad, but if you want to free yourself so that you can have this ever-present flow, these are the awarenesses that you will come to.)

Freeing the emotional means that one comes to the point where he says, "I don't want to be dissipating my energies into anger, fear, etc." This awakening causes one to realize how much energy is wasted in having opinions, biases and attachments.

### *Depression*

Let's begin with the most difficult emotional symptom — depression. I see depression as the end result of a prolonged period of undefined or unacknowledged emotional activity in the body. Often we choose to ignore or repress an emotion inside us until the strain has diminished the body's energy so excessively that the whole system must shut down to protect itself. At that point, we manifest all the symptoms — low energy, mental fatigue and depression.

For example, you are in a state of depression. All of your energy is pressed inward rather than outward, you are lost in yourself; something is wrong, you know it, but you don't know how to get out. This can be the result of emotions going unnoticed and keeping your energy low.

To work with this aspect of depression, we need to know how to experience those unrecognized emotions or those that are too big for us to dare to let in. How can one experience emotions in a very general sense?

First, you must become keenly aware of your feelings which are the internal senses that express as emotions. You are living in a high-powered, high-speed world. Your child comes to you and is involved in an action or statement that affects you; maybe you don't feel the feeling of hurt or anger towards your child because you have been taught not to feel those things. This goes on over a long period of time, and gradually you become a person who is never aware of any feelings moving through you. Not being aware of your feelings is suppression. Repression occurs when you decide a feeling is "not okay" and say to yourself, "I won't let myself feel that."

It is important to know a feeling is present, but it is not necessary to put a label on it. All feeling is life energy either expressed and manifested or blocked. Excessive blocking creates depression. I suggest you become aware of your internal experience and watch it move through you without attaching to it.

### Labeling

How do you come to know and experience a feeling? The minute you feel it in your body, you actually are experiencing it. You don't even have to label the feeling, for you are close to it in knowing it in your body, your senses, and thoughts. You will feel sadness moving like a warm something that comes over you and feel crying coming through. Loneliness will ooze into your sensory system; joy will exhilarate and stimulate your adrenalin. This is called "becoming" and then, gradually, "being aware."

At this point of being aware of the feeling, my suggestion is that you be with it. "Being with" is closer to the experience than labeling.

You can take all kinds of courses to gain awareness, either in groups or classes. We must first go through a process of identifying a feeling and then eventually moving beyond labeling it.

We start by identifying. "Oh, that knot inside me has been hurting for a long time." You have to go through the learning to shed the label. Start being aware when something happens and feel it in your body, senses, or mind. You may say, "I hurt, that hurts, I feel hurt."

Some people consider awareness of a feeling to be, "Well, I wonder if I have been hurt?" "I think I must be sad; I wonder if I'm lonely." Such attempts are actually analyses, too near the surface and removed from one's self-knowledge.

### *Transforming Emotion*

Once you become aware of feelings, it is possible to short-cut emotions; this is not usually taught. The tendency today is to teach not to suppress or repress. Instead, become aware and live out your feelings, emotionalize them. That is fine at one stage; but this can be speeded up. Therefore we teach people to become aware of a feeling, be with it in the moment, and then let it transform itself. Transformation means instead of extending it or emitting the feeling, "let it go." This raises the emotional energy automatically.

For example, joy is high energy and depression is low energy. When we get into feelings that we don't like, we feel pulled down, so something in us "drops out". Loneliness comes in, and you can feel yourself drop; fear comes in, and you feel yourself panic; rage comes in, and suddenly you are absorbed into the thing you are mad at. You CAN do something else at these moments.

For instance, some incident happens "to you", caused by the outside world. The tendency and training today is to take this incident that happened via the outside person, place or thing, recognize it, let it express, feel it, until it takes over and completes itself when finished. It takes you over because you give it power through thought and feeling energy, as a result of your beliefs, life experiences and conditionings. You become lost in feeling. However, you can be sure that feelings gradually play themselves out, end, dissipate. For instance, you will gradually come out of depression. You will. Be very careful not to hold yourself in it, because you will come out of it. Everything in the Universe changes, so you too will change, given enough time.

If you have learned enough about your own feelings, you know that they can take you over, absorb you, take up your mind, your time, your energy. Many people tire of feelings being the theme of their life, running them. I am suggesting that if you're one of those, there is something else you can do. At the point where you have let yourself be with a feeling and have been caught up in it, you can focus on not allowing that energy to drop down; ask it, instead, to move up. That is all there is to it. You don't let your mind get scattered into the thing; you don't get into analysis; you don't try to figure it out; you don't try to understand where it came from, or what it is. You don't go through any of those processes. You don't even have to figure out why your husband makes you angry, or go back and look at what his mother did to him that makes him respond to you the way he does — none of that. You just become aware, "I am angry."

If you have moved to that point in your life where you don't want to waste yourself being angry any more or waste your life in this way, then you can invite yourself to NOT get into it. But you do that after you are aware — and that is all the difference there is in raising emotional energy and repression. Gradually you become detached.

Some people think that we teach repression. We do not, because we teach you to be aware first. Doing this entire process of watching and detaching will take time and courage. You have not been trained or conditioned for this. Most of us believe we deserve our feelings, they are righteous and protective. I understand that. Regardless, we can shortcut and let them transform us if we want another way of being.

## LIFESTYLE/ENVIRONMENT

The last area from which one must become free is lifestyle and environment. Increasingly, I realize that developing the spiritual life must be done in a certain kind of atmosphere. For instance it is more difficult in the big cities. The rural life, the country life, open space, provides an atmosphere in which these attitudes have a better chance to grow. Once developed, it is easier to live them out in a more active life.

I know you cannot do this work in an environment where your relationships are tearing and wearing. For a long time I tried to prove the "law of love" in my life, allowing people to do whatever they wanted in reference to me, a belief that I was really working with. They could hurt me, let me down, take all they wanted — to me, that proved my capacity to love. That was what I was learning at that time. It has gradually moved to the point where I am aware that in terms of intimate relationships, my right environment must have in it those people who are of a similar consciousness.

It is possible to walk in the midst of thousands of people and be a light. But where you live and where you put your body, and the consciousness that you put it in, must be synchronistic and harmonious. Don't fool yourselves; don't damage yourselves; don't play with proving how loving you are or how much you can put up with. If you do, it will cost in developing spiritually. You may have to make a choice in values, but make it clearly.

## *SUMMARY*

Let's close this section by giving a glimpse of the process.

I am born as pure Spirit. I learn to relate to the world from those around me. I am fed thoughts, actions, reactions, an expected way of performing and doing. Someone else teaches me: when to cry, when not to cry; what is bad, what is good; when to go fast, when to go slow. I am even taught a sequential way of thinking. I take all of this in; it becomes my world. As I grow up, I relate to the world as I have been taught. I re-enact it; I keep projecting it out upon all life.

Experiences come into my world; I may learn or not learn. I continue to perpetuate the feelings, the reactions, the movements, the responses and beliefs. Somewhere along the way, in any life, all of this says "halt". That may be the greatest change in one's life.

We may call it "mid-life change," "postpartum depression," "alcoholism," "jilted". Yet, if we talk about this spiritually, we could say that it is time for this life change in the person. It is one of the most beautiful ways to look at such a massive change. You couldn't take it anymore!

You could no longer be motivated by buying more T.V. sets, sailing to the Bahamas next summer, flying to Africa next winter.

It is time for this crack in your "cosmic egg". When it cracks, you fall down. Your whole structure is pulled from underneath you. So there

you stand with you, with no tools to cope with this shift, because you have only been taught to think linearly. Who of us has learned to feel awareness or change awareness?

You may find that you have had feeling and emotional experiences throughout your life, which went unnoticed. Now they are all starting to come out. You are hoping you will make it, as your life falls down around you. You may have tremendous reactions. You may find you cannot control your emotions. They express everywhere. That will change, too. The price of emotion is exhaustion, fatigue, inability to concentrate, general low energy, and an inability to function. You start asking, "What can I do about this? I've opened up; I've become vulnerable; I've exposed myself for whatever reason." Some people are forced into the experience because of their jobs, their love relationships, a change in lifestyle — it doesn't matter. You will get tired of it because it has its natural end as well. You do come to that moment when you say, "This has to stop! I've had enough!"

When that happens, there is another step in the process. You begin to sense that there is a way to be larger than usual humanness. There is a way that is freer, easier. You start saying, "I don't want to give all of me away to these reactions." You start shoring up your seeing, you start putting some "straight" lines in again, and you start rebuilding your structure from a deeper, internal place. Not a place conditioned by the outside world, but one which comes from you — not you the Rebel, but you the Knower. You do this because you are the one who said "halt." You really said "halt" earlier when you fell apart, but you did not know it; you do not find out that you said "halt" until you find yourself wiped out. Then when you realize it, you say, "And now I am going to learn how to build myself in my world."

At this time you have to start filling in some solid places. You may just add a neck, metaphorically, and it may take six months to shape that neck, but you add it. Maybe the neck is called, "I am the authority in here." Then you may add another body part such as, "I am not going to give myself away to anything or anyone." So you now move into a situation where somebody appears to be able to pull you off center. You can feel that power start to go out and you hear inside, "Wait a minute! I have an inner authority in my life that says I will not give myself away to any person, place or thing — they do not have power in my life." So you pull it all back in, and it may take you four hours, but you have made a decision that it is not worth the cost, you are not going to live emotionally spent. You may find that this happens partially. You experience your heart beginning to go out to someone to whom you are attracted: you want to get involved, and you hear, "Wait a minute, come back inside, I am not sure I want to relate in that old way." You may have brief fantasies; I had all kinds of fantasies during that period of time, like, "I know - I am going to get a new job, that's what I'll do to change this thing." Then I'd say, "Wait a minute, is that it?" I would bring it back inside and wait a little bit longer.

I think the whole consciousness then goes through a change. You find that you have come through this shift as a person with a whole new set of goals and ideals. Before I went into this period, I was totally goal-oriented. I was totally propelled. It was a beautiful thing to watch, for me anyway and apparently for a whole bunch of others, too. But it couldn't go on; it had to stop. I never thought about things I think about now. Now I think about consciousness. Then all I thought about was the Center, building new buildings and getting more people to come here. Now I am excited about watching consciousness grow and how I can assist it. In one sense I am doing what I am here to do. Your structure rebuilds and you emerge a new person. A different inner being has formed, one whose reality is now inside and integrated.

Remember, nobody is right or wrong on this journey. Everybody is finding his own way. I do not want to set myself up to say that anything I am doing is the way. Not at all! I only believe in the process, and I find that the process is definitely one of diminishing one's possessions. That went against my whole belief system, which was to get bigger and better, my whole American dream system which is to do more, not to do less, to have more, not to have less. For me, personally, that diminishing process is going to continue, because as the concept grows me, I keep waking up to how I am misusing the earth's resources.

So, for example, I want to use much less electricity. I want to cooperate with the nature of my planet, so I see that most of my excess has to go. I want fewer things to have to take care of because it is the only thing I can do. I understand Thoreau's[12] statement about the three pieces of marble in his home which required his dusting them, and thereby, he realized caring for his possessions took time away from tending his own soul. For me to be removing myself from worldly involvement is a total reverse, but it is the only thing I can do. That does not mean everybody has to do it that way. For many others, now is their time to go out into the world.

The way is different for each of us. However, though different ways bring us to similar realizations, I still do not believe you can mistreat your body, dissipate your emotions, keep running

---

[12] Henry David Thoreau, *Walden and Civil Disobedience*, "I had three pieces of limestone on my desk, but was terrified to find they required to be dusted daily, when the furniture of my mind was all undusted still, and I threw them out the window."

at mental high speed, or live in a negative environment and expect to experience this state you desire. I am suggesting that when this realization of something powerful, available and imminent touches you, a way to experience it more fully is to let go of the attachments that shroud you from it.

# 3: UNDERSTANDING SPIRITUAL GROWTH

## *ASPIRATION: THE WHY OF THE SPIRITUAL PATH*

### *A DEFINITION*

As one conscious of your own spiritual path, no doubt you have asked the question, "Why am I on a Spiritual path?" or "What do I think I am doing?"

Many have discovered answers that refer to feeling a "sense", "a longing to know", "a hungering", or something moving you into a previously unrecognized path. What causes such drive, such movement, such forceful changes in human thinking and behavior?

The answer comes when one acknowledges that born into every human being is a seed not only for physical growth, but also for physiological, emotional and mental growth. Also born into every human being is an inherent sense of aspiration. The word "aspire" comes from the

Latin spiro, which means "to breathe". It is derived from the word "inspire", which is used poignantly in the second chapter of Genesis. There it states that God leaned over man and breathed into him the breath of life. Inspire means to breathe in, to draw in; aspire means to move toward. The sense is that God inspires us and we aspire toward God. That inherent, aspiring drive is the signal of the soul's growing and pushing its way more obviously into conscious awareness. When it appears, it must be responded to — thus the spiritual path is initiated within the human being.

I do not know how to communicate how integral this is except to say, it is there. We cannot avoid it; it is so obvious that it is not even special in an ultimate sense — it is there.

The fact is that we are all on "the path". Some simply are more conscious of it than others and define it as a "Spiritual" path. It seems to take on Spiritual definition when the individual becomes conscious and aware of it. The soul has spoken inwardly and can no longer be denied.

The way to explore this element of aspiration within yourself is to observe it in your life and notice its particular quality. I have often seen it move in my life as it expanded and completed, expanded and completed again. Once something completes itself, it is as if something else arises out of it. After that which "arises" out of itself has expanded, it tops over. At the point when it tops and begins to close in, something new moves out of it automatically.

There is much symbolism throughout man's heritage that represents his awareness of this. Chardin teaches of it in "*The Phenomenon of Man*"[13]. He states that throughout evolution, new growth has moved out, closed itself in after expansion; then in that moment, just at the very tiny point before complete closure, something moves in and expands out again. Chardin calls these forms "peduncles."

The same can be seen in the first chapters of Genesis which describe creation. Just at that point where creation is completed and God rests, man is created. After involution in the first chapter, evolution occurs in the second chapter in the form of man. This process is happening to us throughout our lives. It is as if we cannot avoid the activity of God within us. We call this growth,

---

[13] Pierre Teilhard De Chardin, *The Phenomenon of Man* (New York: Harper & Row, Publishers, 1959)

"graduation from high school and college" and "getting married". Then we call it "bearing our first child", "having our first job", "economic security". Then when that tide closes in, we may call it "a feeling of completion in the community in which one begins to care for others".

As we progress through these stages of our lives and satisfy their requirements, we begin to develop our own "security triangle". As defined by Abraham Maslow[14], this is the state in which we find ourselves when all of the "basics" have been met. In this state we experience spiritual reflection.

This does not mean that spirituality has not always been present, but that we now have a better chance to observe it. Why? Because all the mundane, material, practical aspects of our existence have been taken care of. Once these are taken care of, a person can reflect upon his life process and its intention. That activity of self-reflection is God within.

---

[14] Abraham Maslow's theory on "Hierarchy of Needs" proposed in 1943.

## REVIEW

The spiritual path exists because the sense of aspiration is inborn, just as the form of the body is inborn. This aspiration is a movement that is undeniable, ever-present, and usually not obvious early in life.

In most people, it is a forgotten thread, lying in the background. While caught up in the material world, they do not observe it, nor call their own life activity God. However, when the material world begins to lose its power and is completed, then we begin to observe and hunger for the activity of Spirit. It has always been there, but now one seeks to identify and clarify it.

The Spiritual part of us is so powerful that if something hinders us so that this movement cannot penetrate through us, death takes place. Spirituality is so powerful that I am sure this is the reason suicide occurs. Suicides do not occur as an affirmation of death; they occur as a statement that "I could not get any more life, and I could not live without more life."

In fact, death is Spirit energy blocked; the understanding was not big enough to incorporate the next growth, the next expansion. In line with this, when each of us is born, we have a soft spot that is closed in. I have always felt that my search involved a push at that same place at the top of my head, a push to get out again. That push is the aspiring energy. When well-developed yogis die, they consciously push themselves through that same place at the top of the head, I would assume it gradually opens again because all the other channels and chakras are clear, and the energy can once again leave the body.

I have only mentioned humans having aspiration within them. I am convinced as well, that every material form, from the atom on, has aspiration within it. Because of this aspiration, evolution has occurred. In other words, when I look at my dog, I do not think that Cindy is done; she is evolving. Sometimes she acts so human that I can almost feel her jumping into my place on the totem pole, and I do happen to believe that humans are the present top of that evolutionary totem pole.

### POINT OF DEPARTURE

The final understanding I would communicate regarding aspiration is that we only become conscious of being on a spiritual path when we have completed and integrated four major parts of ourselves; when we have taken care of our economic needs by caring for the physical body, home and job; when we have taken care of our self-identity and personality so we know who we are; when we have taken care of relationships and know how to love; and when we have taken care of our relationship to the earth. Unless you feel that you have responded to these areas and fulfilled their obligations in your life, I do not think it is possible to live fully Spiritual.

I used to think a person could leap over, cut through, or leave out aspects of their development in some areas. Spirit only becomes full when all those parts are whole and right within us, and that feeling of rightness comes when we are detached from each of those essentials. As an example, we have fulfilled our economic need when it is no longer a drive or force that worries or concerns us.

I can use myself as an example. After I sold my house in 1980, someone said, "Well, were you sad?" I said, "No it just seems as if I sold my house." It was strange, for when I realized the house was gone, I said to my realtor, "I have fears that I'll get depressed; maybe I'll think I did the wrong thing." But none of that happened. "Where are you going to live when you move?" I said, "I will probably just sit on somebody's porch." I can really see myself doing that. It doesn't seem to matter. One becomes detached.

Such detachment occurs, too, in love relationships. In other words (and this is obviously difficult to do), the person whom you love, or whom you are living with, can say, "I am leaving tomorrow because I have fallen in love with somebody else," and you can say, "I rejoice." Such rejoicing is not an indication of non-caring or hidden anger or naiveté, but rather an "order of rightness" for each person. Such detachment would have occurred in all four areas so a person felt free and yet, strangely, connected with all.

## INDICATORS OF THE ASPIRING MOVEMENT

The Spiritual path exists because of man's immutable nature to aspire, to breathe towards God. It is an evolutionary part of everyone's life which becomes more obvious as we integrate our physical needs, clarify our self-identity, understand relationships, and care for the earth.

### CATALYSTS

Another cause for the movement of aspiration may be the influence of some catalytic agent. A particular catalyst may enter as a protrusion out of nowhere and stop, or radically alter, everything else. Sometimes experienced as a "crisis" such as a disease or a relationship ceasing or changing, it forces a person to look deeper for the strength and a larger dimension to handle the experience.

Other catalytic agents might be "life changes" themselves. Many teachers have noted that these changes occur in increments of seven; age 7, 14, 28, etc. Such a change does not occur because of a crisis, but because a person's system shifts.

Your system, your life, the "seed" of you, has its own inner timetable. We might say "God and Mother Nature both have their own timetables." At certain points in your life, all former ways of being and doing come to a halt, strangely, abruptly, and without apparent cause. For years you might have moved with poise and great ego power and in one day, one instant, it all shifts, and you are plunged into confusion, limbo, nothingness. From such a shift comes the "search" for God, an awareness of the aspiration within you, and the necessity for a new birth.

A third such catalytic agent is probably the most frightening of all — encountering the possibility of no longer being around. It is probably the most powerful and the ugliest experience. It is often described as "nothingness" or emptiness. That is how it first appeared to me, as a huge pull. The only way I can describe what was happening was that something was pulling me out of existence, and as a result, I was forced to see my true loneliness, emptiness, insignificance, and lack of meaning. This force is such a powerful part of all human nature that it led to the whole study of existential philosophy and psychology. This deep human recognition is at the very core of us, a sense this recognition does not necessarily come from the fact that you are getting older or that you are going to die or anything related. It is just something that appears.

## *THE IDENTITY CRISIS*

Life is like walking along a roadway which has scenes, nuances, and experiences to address. None of us can avoid these experiences however hard we try to hide them, cover them up or run from them. You are going to grow up; you are going to get older, and one of the most poignant encounters will be with the reality, the existence, of your own nothingness.

With it comes an old question with a new meaning: "Who am I?" At this point, the "Who am I" question transforms itself from that of a thirteen or fourteen-year-old child whose question is: "Who am I in relation to society?" At this point, the "Who am I" question becomes: "Who am I eternally?"

We talk about the self-identity crisis. That "crisis" with regard to jobs, circumstances and relationships is a very different matter than "Who am I?" in terms of my essence as a living being. It is this latter question that must be answered.

Many people, who encounter this existential nothingness, run away from it. My mother bumped into it in 1960. I watched her go through a tremendous struggle. I didn't know how to serve her; I didn't even know what was happening, nor did she or anyone who attempted to help her. Today, I do know.

About five years ago, my mother told me that if she had not been with my father (whom she felt a bond to care for), and if she could have worked with herself spiritually, she would have broken through the encounter but instead, she has taken tranquilizers, off and on, ever since. Why? To keep calm, tranquil, faced with the huge vacuum opening up, faced with feeling empty and alone.

Many of you know of a big hole opening up inside; many people have used drugs to cope with it — from heavy drugs to light aspirin. Drugs can be an attempt to cover and avoid the great void inside.

## THE DARK NIGHT

This state of nothingness is often called "the dark night of the soul." Every saint has known it and has had the courage to survive it. It is called a dark night because suddenly one is "just sitting there," and something vast and empty opens up. You become vulnerable.

My statement to myself while going through this was, "Just keep opening up. Be willing to be vulnerable. Keep being more and more vulnerable; there is nothing to fear, there is nothing to fear."

"Oh, yes there is!" I would answer back.

Then again, courageously, I would hear, "Open up. Trust. The fear is a natural response to the unknown."

When that space opens up, we get extremely scared, so we try to close it down again. One of the ways we try to close it down is to lose ourselves in our emotions. Many of us get angry or jealous because we don't allow this to open up. I am convinced that all feelings really come from avoiding this space. I got bored with my whole emotional system a few years ago. It didn't turn me on anymore; it didn't do me any good, and so in facing this, I saw that it had been a means for me to keep the "hole" filled.

Another way we avoid this space is to talk fast, move fast, and stay high—an experience we have an affinity for in our culture. I was hooked on being high. Most often now I describe myself as flat, uninteresting, not excited, just here. I generally have hated being "just here". Who would want to watch or be with somebody who is "just here?" I know what it is like to look for a high, in fact my whole search has been for the mystical high. When I drove into Colorado recently, I experienced a powerful high. As a result I thought the high must be in Colorado; so then I might go back to that spot and supplicate it and see if I could build a house right there where it happened. Well, you and I know it won't happen. I may be there a year or so and then I'll lose it because it was never there anyway.

Alan Watts states in *"Behold The Spirit"*[15] that everybody is seeking to move through this dimension of existence. He says they are seeking God outside themselves and within the church:

> *"Modern man is indifferent to religion as he knows it. And yet his nervous restlessness, his chronic sense of frustration, his love of sensationalism as an escape, his fitful use of every substitute for religion from state worship to getting*

---

[15] Alan Watts, *Behold the Spirit* (New York: Random House, 1947), p. 9

*drunk, shows that his soul still desires that release from itself, that infusion of light and meaning, through being possessed by a power greater than itself which is found perfectly in union with God alone."*

## ESSENTIAL QUALITIES FOR THE SPIRITUAL PATH

There are four essential qualities for participation in what we call the Spiritual Path: courage, participation, trust and self-love.

### COURAGE

With reference to the first, courage, let's consider an analogy. You walk into a room of people and are told you are going to learn to fly. After superficially exploring man's ability to fly by flapping your arms a few times, the platform on which you are standing is abruptly removed. Imagine your fear. You have suddenly been thrust into the experience of being off the ground for life.[16] Maybe you had only just learned how to be

---

[16] [You have nothing to hang onto; no past experience to help you know what to do; you have no understanding of how to succeed at this and have no idea of how it will end.] ed. Coy F. Cross II

'grounded'. If you are to go on with this experiment, one of the qualities you will need most is courage.[17] And this is not the courage to become famous, or to be good at anything: it is the courage to stand being nothing — to stand it. I used to have an idea of courage which was the "impossible dream" kind of courage, charging windmills in the name of some mission. I was courageous, but when it came down to living with me and not running away from me, I had to do a great deal of learning and growing, to develop a new kind of courage.

One of the most important lines I ever read was by Carl Jung[18], who said that one has to hold on to the ground of their being. I held on to my life. It wasn't with my hand; it was with something else, some new part of me — my soul perhaps. I had to experience over and over again that

---

[17] [You use courage instead of wondering, "What is next?" There is no next. You are here right now. And now, here you are. And a few seconds later, you are here right now. It takes courage to be right here and right now without something to hang on to. And you will need courage to move ahead in each moment with no knowledge of how it will turn out.] ed. Coy F. Cross II

[18] He was a Swiss-born psychiatrist who founded analytical psychology

nothing was wrong; nothing was out of order; everything was fine. You are not holding on to your principles or your position, or asserting your rights. You're holding on to the inner core. You are building the internal part of you.

Earlier in this material, I mentioned the "Who Am I?" question. That 'Who Am I' is what you are holding on to — your essence, your life, the part of you that always is, that always has been and always will be. You are in the process of finding that part of you, so that you will know when you walk in the flame that part of you cannot be burned. That is the only way you learn how to walk in the flame. That part of you is so impervious it cannot be burned and it can make all else holy as well. That part of you cannot be killed.

This feeling of courage is the kind of courage seen in the story of Abraham. When Abraham is told to take his son to be killed, he gets on his donkey and goes forward. He doesn't go forward with the belief that his son will be saved. That is the old Christian teaching of hope and promise. It is the teaching I was raised with: "Go forward and everything will work out. You will get what you want." [19]

But this is a dangerous teaching. It demands certain results. It forces God into a position of conditions; for example, if you do this, then you will prove yourself! This kind of courage I am describing has no demands. It is!

In *"The Courage To Be"*[20], Paul Tillich describes this kind of courage as the courage to go on. And you do go on, not because you will become great, not because you will prove anything, not because you will look good, but just because your life is valuable as it is!

The key to the whole story of Abraham is not that Isaac is saved; the key is that Abraham places his child on the altar.

The end result is not important. There is no great outcome. There is not always a healing. You do not pray for healing; you do not pray for a good

---

[19] [The old Christian teaching of hope and promise is: if you trust God and you pray correctly it will turn out well for you - the way you want it to be resolved.] ed. Coy F. Cross II

[20] Paul Tillich, *The Courage to Be* (New Haven CN: Yale University Press, 1952)

outcome. You have the courage to be with your own life as it is.[21]

## *PARTICIPATION*

The second essential quality is participation. It seems funny to teach on the one hand that the presence of God, Life, Spirit is working in you automatically, that everything is in Divine Order and that you can come to no harm, and then to say, "You have to help." I have always found that difficult to present to others. The question is why do you have to help?

You have to help because you are conditioned to believe you can be harmed. So you have to participate. You have to affirm the rightness of what is happening to you by releasing and letting go of old beliefs through ongoing prayer and meditation.

---

[21] [You have the courage to trust that God is in charge and that things will turn out the way God intended them to turn out. You do what is given you to do without expectation of how it will end. Carol Ruth and I talked about the Abraham story and I asked "Why don't you tell people the message would have been the same if Abraham had sacrificed his son?" She replied, "I don't because they are not ready to hear that." But here in this book she does say it. Perhaps she thought her audience was now ready. ] ed. Coy F. Cross II

## TRUST

Another essential quality is trust. Finally in all events, we must not see accidents but, rather, the hand of God. We believe that we live in a hostile Universe; we must learn that the Universe is benign. God works in all and even penetrates the thoughtless moment. All that is, regardless of appearances, is part of the carefully intended whole. Nothing is wasted. The fact that a parent treats a child badly is neither them, nor the child, but is a part of a perfect plan. The fact that you don't get that precious love that you always thought was so wonderful is nobody's fault; it is not even interference that keeps it from you. It is a loving universe working out life. The fact that your daughter left you is not inimical. That is right process working itself out. That is the belief we must come to.

Minonomas, a second century Arabian monastic, stated:

*"Cease to seek after God as if It were outside of you and the Universe and things similar to those. Seek Him from out of your own self and learn who it is and say, 'My God, my mind, my reason, my soul, my body.' And learn about yourself.*

*And if you will closely investigate all of these things you will find them in yourself."*[22]

### SELF-LOVE

A final issue which must be acknowledged before entering the deeper considerations of the spiritual path is self-love. As you live out your life experience with change, you will find that at the very roots of your struggle is how capable you are of accepting yourself totally.

Just for a moment, ask yourself the question, "Do I love me?"

The first response may be, "Yes. Of course I do."

Well, let's test this further. Do you love and accept yourself when you are down as well as up, absurd as well as intelligent, a failure as well as success, sick as well as healthy? That is the test — to be able to love yourself all the way through, unconditionally. Somehow, we are all learning this constantly. And the depth of the learning extends further and further into your being.

---

[22] E. Kadloabodsky and G.E.H. Palmer, trans., *Writings on the Philokalia on Prayer of the Heart* (London: Faber and Faber Limited, 1992), p. 27

For instance, sometimes when we hear these ideas, we believe we can love ourselves totally as suggested. So we go to work, loving it all. But then we find we cannot love some part of us, the anger or jealousy or lust. We find ourselves resisting this inability to accept. At that point, my recommendation is accept yourself not being accepting. You can see how deep this self-love penetrates then, can't you?

How does one go about loving oneself? You must draw upon the teachings in earlier sections: caring for the body, letting the emotions subside, and developing awareness mentally. The key to self-love occurs as your awareness refines itself. The quicker you can catch self-judgment, the sooner you can see it, the more effective will be the self-loving. When you see it and catch yourself judging you, simply be your own counselor.

You may speak to yourself words like, "It's alright to be as I am now. I am a part of God's universe, and all of me is included, nothing is left out. I join with God in accepting this part of me, too." There is nothing else to do — you don't have to get rid of anything, punish anything, or set anything straight, affirm, or deny. Only trust that God knows what God is doing.

And where does this all lead? Does this kind of license lead to depravity, cruelty, insensitivity? No, not with this kind of base upon which it is founded — belief in God as operator of the Universe.

When you trust and build a life system on this base, loving the "whole" releases energy to be shared, to be given, to be used, to be creative. As the love radiates through the whole system, all becomes embraced by it.

And, as the nature of the Universe, as energy is released through refinement, it expands and evolves along with the rest of the natural order of physics. It is as if a refining fire burns within, and all that comes into its presence is nurtured and expanded. That is self-love.

# 4: ASPECTS OF THE SPIRITUAL PATH

This section presents aspects of the Spiritual Path, such as special effects, dynamics, highs, mystical experiences and enlightenment. As you proceed through this material, it will be helpful to consult the Process Model at the end of the chapter.

## THE PROCESS

### NOT-CONSCIOUS

We begin with the stage of being "not-conscious". I believe that many people spend an entire lifetime not conscious. My only explanation for that is in reincarnation, understanding that people are continually evolving now, just as life has evolved historically and geologically. Just because we are all human beings does not mean that we are all at the same place in evolution. Some are still at the conscious level of the Neanderthal Man.

A not-conscious person is someone who lives at the instinctual level. Much of their nature and behavior functions from the instinctual carryover of genes and heritage. For instance, Cindy, my dog, functions instinctually. If I harm her, she bites me. Through my evolution, I realize that she is protecting herself, and not to respond by smashing her back. If I did, I would be functioning at the same instinctual level, I believe I am intended to be more refined than my dog, and I had to work with that. The first time she bit me, my nose turned black and blue. I could feel the rage. As I raised my hand, I could see how much power I was getting out of that moment and that realization stopped me. Then I held her and I saw that it is her right to defend herself.

Functioning at a not-conscious, instinctual level means being caught up in self, survival, and taking care of our system's lower needs. The not-conscious may be very aware of what they are doing, about what they are trying to accomplish, and why they are attempting to get there. It is not wrong: it just is.

Surprisingly, it is possible for a very religious person to be not-conscious. Such people will seek churches which support such non-consciousness, churches that found their teachings on judging others, making their opinions and beliefs superior to others, and oppressing the wrong-doers or non-believers. Such non-conscious behavior by highly intelligent individuals was explained thoroughly in Jung's "shadow theory". The anti-Semitism in World War II is a classic example of non-consciousness projected onto an entire society.

This not-conscious state in larger group is often reflected by those who oppose abortion or support equal rights or those who find power in condemnation and opposition.

## *CONSCIOUS*

After living in a not-conscious stage for a certain period of time, being conscious starts to appear with internal questions like, "Why am I doing that? What about somebody else?" Another way the conscious state begins is in self-doubt about all former beliefs. Such an intrusion of inner thoughts and attitudes can be difficult, grey, even dark, because the whole being is shifting.

Being conscious means seeing oneself as having the capacity to control and to manifest whatever one desires. One feels powerful as they see and experience that they can create.

Such control, mastery and use of one's hands and body to win and manifest in the world has an attractive, even spiritual, quality to it. Conquering, mastery and overcoming go with becoming conscious and accepting responsibility. Such words as "I am master" have high appeal. Those words surely appeal to me. Remember the poem, "I am the master of my fate, the captain of my soul."?[23] Such

---

[23] William Ernest Henley, "Invictus", written in 1875.

powerful realizations create religions like Unity, organizations like EST[24], new programs that develop self-belief. This is a stage where one understands and lives dynamically that wonderful word "Assertion".

With the conscious stage come activities like working with affirmations and denials. One takes success-motivation courses, reads books like *"Think and Grow Rich"*[25] and *"Psycho-Cybernetics"*[26] and re-programs their whole mental and emotional system to be successful, dynamic and powerful. One might create a treasure map, using pictures and bold words to image what one wants or wants to become. All these processes are powerful and effective. I still use them at times, but now I understand all the dynamics, the possibilities and the risks and attitudes involved, which can cause despair and hopelessness when they do not always work.

---

[24] Erhard Seminars Training, by Werner Erhard

[25] Napoleon Hill, *Think and Grow Rich* (New York: Penguin Books, 2003).

[26] Maxwell Maltz, *Psycho-Cybernetics* (New York: Penguin Books, 1960).

Such issues must be addressed on the spiritual journey.

## PASSAGE

This conscious stage has its life also, just as everything has its life. Soon it, too, ends. This occurs when one reaches the place where all of this conscious creation loses its power, its appeal, and its interest. Something comes along and says, "Halt! You cannot push that anymore, you cannot get bigger and better for the rest of your life. That is not all that life is about".

I recently had a visit by a minister from the region who had thrown his back out. He said to me, "Well, it's going to get better". I looked at him and said, "John, the muscle spasm is the activity of your body doing what it must do. Don't try to 'get better'; be with it!" I no longer try to overcome life. I don't try to get through anything.

In the conscious stage one overcomes. As one approaches the next stage, acceptance is the key. It has always surprised me that this "stop" does not happen to everybody, and I would presume the reason is that it is a matter of individual evolution and not everyone enters here.

When I entered this period I experienced a wall through which I could not pass. I felt hurt, an entirely new kind of hurt, not personal. It was a life hurt that brought forth anguish, despair, a feeling of loss and loneliness having nothing to do with material goods lost nor loneliness from people. This was of the soul, a clearly difficult sensation. I had been master of the ship, creator, expressor, victor, and I could no longer function that way. The old system did not work, and it ceased overnight. Frankly, it was a time of pure wonder, wonderful although I only experienced initial shock and horror.

You have heard all those statements: "Get up off the floor!" "Get back in the ring". "Don't go down for the ten-count" — the great statements that many of us have lived by. Yet, every time you get up this time, in this passage, you get kicked and you are doing nothing different than before, but now it doesn't work.

The reason this is happening is that the former conscious way is finished. The fully conscious way, which is a most glorious adventure, is completed. This conscious stage has led to success, power, magnetism, and charisma. It has been all the great, dramatic lines of victory, going forward, conquering, and winning. But when life says, "Stop" and the former conscious way is left; then enters the famous dark night of the soul. We all have to recognize and appreciate that the mystics, and frankly anybody who has stepped into a new inner life, have experienced the dark night of the soul.

The politician may say, "I had to abandon running for office"; the athlete will say, "I hung up my gloves"; the drunkard says, "I hit bottom"; the emotional fireball says, "I couldn't get up anymore"; the person who has been sexually powerful says, "I became impotent".

They are indicators of the passage into the dark night. One's integrity, one's courage, will determine whether the passage will lead forward into expansion or collapse into maintaining a former consciousness state. It is a great potential moment in the inner journey.

### THE DARK NIGHT

What, then, is the nature of the stage called "the dark night of the soul"? How do you know when, or if, you have reached that stage?

I will never forget this stage in my own life. I had searched for a definition, a name, for what I was going through. I knew it wasn't "burnout". I knew I wasn't ill, but something was definitely amiss. I came back from Hawaii after a three month sabbatical in 1977, and went to my dissertation advisor. She said she wanted me to do my dissertation on my recent experience, to use my dissertation to find a way through. She gave me *"Dark Night of the Soul"*, by Saint John of the Cross[27]. In it I found a passage that said, "When your fantasies, even your meditations, your aspirations, even your thoughts stop."

I read that passage and I knew, "That's me — all I had known had stopped!" Once discovered and named, I chose to live it out and let it lead me to the next part of my life.

The dark night of the soul is the experience where the hole opens up. It is a powerful state that one must allow oneself to go into. Most people fight it. But entering it is the only way through. The main message as one goes through is to realize it is all right. That is all you have to do; keep knowing "it is alright!" This

---

[27] St. John of the Cross, *The Dark Night of the Soul* (Trowbridge, Wiltshire GB: Redwood Press Limited, 1973).

process, this feeling, is right. This emptiness, this void, this pit is right; it is right on!

This experience is the same as that which occurs in the birth canal for the birth of a child. The same void is seen in pre-birth pictures of a child preparing for birth, it is process; it is unavoidable. When you are being born physically, you go through it, although not consciously.

In the course of every day you go through such voids as well. When you say, "I am low in energy" or, "I am down," a natural process of your system is occurring to shut you off, to protect you. In the dark night experience, rather than a small lull in the system, a vast chasm is opening to prepare you for a whole new world of consciousness. You must only learn how to paddle the boat as you go through these greyish, foggy, dimly-lit waters.

Why does this dark night happen? As preparation and entrance into another realm of consciousness, and designed into it is the capacity to emerge on the other side. Another word used for this stage is the black hole. Itzhak Bentov explains it clearly in "*Stalking The*

*Wild Pendulum*".[28] A little energy ball, all curled inside itself and moving at high speed, expands out, pushes itself out, and after it has expanded as far as it can, it hits a point where it cannot go any further. That is life. The experience is not something to be overcome; there is nothing to affirm about, nothing to look "for" God about, nothing to get rid of or correct. There is nothing wrong. This energy which has expanded out as far as it can, then fans around, losing momentum, turns in upon itself and slows down.

This is an explanation of the mystical process as well. Then it enters into a black hole where it rebuilds its energy and comes out as a white hole. Black holes always lead to white holes to black holes to white holes to black holes to white holes to black holes. It is the science of the Universe and of the self. And what is coming out the other end, what is that stage mystically? It is a stage of beingness.

I describe this stage as being "consciously not

---

[28] Itzhak Bentov, *Stalking the Wild Pendulum: On the Mechanics of Consciousness* (New York: American Elsevier Publishers, Inc., 1977).

conscious!" Bentov's "black hole theory" supports the peduncle concept of Chardin.[29] Notice the similarity of both models to that of the Process Model presented at the end of this chapter.

The dark night of the soul is the death of the self, the self that has been built. This process of death and decomposition is always going on. Every time you have built anything, it has gone through a similar process.

You fall in love with someone; that love becomes conscious, the lights "go on," a marvelous, mystical marriage occurs. Then, all of a sudden, the "thing" collapses and you enter a dark hole, and you come out a new person.

The death of the self happens in many areas whether they be economic, physical, emotional or other. The dark night of the soul is a massive self-death over a period of time. When that has happened, one moves into a state of "beingness".

---

[29] Pierre Teilhard De Chardin, *The Phenomenon of Man.*

Moving into beingness has a feeling of release that comes with it. Some people mention that they feel they have touched Spirit when they feel this release. Notice the similarities again to the physical birth experience, for once having given birth, the release sensation is profound. Some people mention feeling pain the closer they get to their sense of Spirit — that pain is the dark night. That pain is the point mentioned earlier, where expansion has closed in and is then forced to push itself through a very small space. This space is the point where everything we believed in gets squashed; one feels closed off, and it hurts. It is the ego dying, just before the explosion into being, release, and freedom.

Ego is still present of course, and personality, too. It is so decreased, barely a flicker, and yet there is an entirely new security within. In the state of beingness, the tendency is to want to be quiet. The tendency is to want to discover stillness. My personal knowing has become that, if I can be still long enough, if I cannot be rattled by other personalities (not because personalities turn me off but rather because personalities have always turned me on), if I can keep myself from giving off my energy into the lower areas of my nature, then gradually I can feel the mystical bursts build and move through me.

It is like the peduncles: the quiet is the small, narrow space that then expands as new energy, clearly moves into me, pushing me into another level of experience.

## INTEGRATING THE LIFE ENERGY

Here is a more complete explanation of building and integrating. The physical body has seven chakras or energy spots: one at the base of the spine, one in the genitals, the solar plexus, the heart, the throat, the third eye, and the crown. This explanation comes from an awareness of using the human energy system to work in behalf of elevating the entire consciousness. It can even lead to mystical periods. In order to experience the mystical state of unification over long periods of time, all parts must be integrated — physical, sexual, emotional, and mental. And each must have been fully used, understood and not blocked or repressed in their expression.

As you develop and observe your being work, as life moves along in you, as you become more aware, you may begin to realize that you do not want to dissipate your life energy into lower chakras. You may see yourself not wanting to let energy into excessive sexual expression; in fact, you may find your self-interest diminishing. You may wonder what is wrong with you: "I don't relate sexually as I used to. My sexual responses do not activate as they used to when meeting a fine looking man or woman. What is missing? That is how I used to know that I loved or was attracted".

Or, as the movement shifts into the higher chakras, thoughts might be heard internally such as, "I don't get angry any more. That or this does not draw my attention anymore". Then may come haunting fear saying, "Oh, God, I must be dead; I must be burned out; people say that only if you're feeling are you alive. Am I all done?" And you live out that fear, watching, waiting, and trusting. As you live it out, as you live out each fear, and watch with courage, you see the fears drop away. Then, amazingly, they don't arise anymore. Not because they were beaten down or affirmed and denied away but because their time came, ended, and they passed on. Sensitivity refines the entire system to recognize what will distract this powerful, wonderful aspiring Life Energy.

Let it be clear, I'm not suggestion you do this — the process itself will do it in you! And remember that these words are not coming from a damaged, hurt person. I do not feel repressed or hung up. They come from one who has lived life fully. They come from understanding, clarity and appreciation of life. I was moved to these decisions and had no control over them once they started. I had done all the studying, begun my doctorate, and lived a full and rich life. Only then did these experiences start working in my system. I would assume that is what is required.

### BEINGNESS

The way I describe the state of beingness is that the role of the personality greatly diminishes and with it the comfortable, more easily known areas of one's existence.

It has been scary for me to be in the state of beingness. At times it has seemed that my feeling nature had become lost entirely, and yet that is not so. I used to feel like a sunburst, and now I feel like a light. I used to enjoy being a sunburst, and it has been hard to give up that splendid experience.

I have had to search for writings and fellow travelers who could provide answers for this strange state. I have come to realize that it is an adjustment to another way of being, a quieter, more contemplative state of being; one more intimate with God.

I was obviously attached to being a sunburst, and yet I did not know this until it was not present anymore. Being is very, very quiet and that has been painful at least for me, to be as quiet as I have become. Why? Because I no longer have the forces to draw upon that I used to count on. I do not draw upon the emotional energy that used to fire me, nor the aggression, nor the sexual energy, nor the passion.

As this quietness has become a part of my personality, I have watched others respond to it. They indicate that they miss my attention, my involvement with them and my response to their ego. Apparently I do not serve them in the old way, either, just as I have felt lost to myself. What is increasingly clear to me is that capacity within me to serve ego, whether mine or someone else's, is diminishing as the self dies.

A word has been paraphrased for this state, "passionlessness". Before you jump in fear at this word, as I first did, read about it, study it, investigate it, to perceive its truth.[30]

As one moves along in this process, he/she begins to make decisions to participate in the refining and defining of the movement of this energy. Since the energy is not being allowed to descend into the lower chakras, it becomes available for expansion and ascension. Remember, no one can do this unless they are ready. We have proved this throughout religious history. Growth itself is pushing this process. Nobody else can! This is not anything to "go for" — please don't get that out of this material, that now you want to "go for" being. Remember, finally it does not matter, and only if it doesn't matter is it allowed to move along.

## *THE GOAL*

"Being" is a state of being "consciously not conscious". A good analogy for this is to follow the development of a concert pianist (and of course I draw upon this because of my having been a concert pianist). A person comes to the

---

[30] Jacob Needleman, *Lost Christianity: A Journey of Rediscovery* (New York: Doubleday & Co., 1980), pp. 22-23.

point of wanting to play the piano. At this point we could call the person "not conscious" for they have no idea what it will involve. The process begins with preparation. Music is put in front of the young child and while sitting at the piano, he/she learns to take the notes from the music and put them through the fingers onto the keyboard. First one looks up at the notes and then down to the hands without being able to be separate from looking at the keys. Then one day, the student is able to look at the music and interpret through his hands without translating notes to keys. That is an important moment — at that point, it could be said, he/she becomes conscious.

Then the student goes to a new teacher and this teacher shows how to develop the body, mind and emotional system, to take the music and allow it to express through the piano and the fingers as the original creative intention. This is done over and over, until he/she makes it to a concert stage and plays for crowds. In front of the audience, he/she experiences fear of forgetting the music and making mistakes. All the time, in the back of the student's mind is a supreme desire to be able to sit at the instrument and let the music play through him/her. Then one day, in the middle of a concert, there is one brief minute when the student forgets him/herself, forgets the audience, and there is a direct line between the music moving through him/her into the piano and out into the concert hall. Such a moment is "nirvana," sought forever after, always.

This analogy shows the not conscious becoming conscious, and finally, consciously not conscious.

When I used to perform publicly, people would come up to me afterwards and mention some passage which sounded like gold. I knew that was the point where I had been free. At that point in the music, something ignited in me and I was out of the way and it burned through me. Everybody knew it.

The goal of life is to be able to be out there for the whole concert with you out of the way. The mind is gone and you become the music. That is the process. That is what we all want to do with living; we do not have to think it through, emote it through; it just goes through. What we forget is that we do not just do that. We first become a conscious participant in it, and then it can happen.

## 5: CONSCIOUSNESS

Now, let's move to recognizing what within us is "working us", "expanding us", and "growing us". It is called consciousness. Consciousness is that part of us within, the part we are hoping to ignite and catalytically charge - to fire up.

I stated earlier that oftentimes people are thrown into seeking a relationship with God by a crisis in their lives. That event becomes the trigger to fire the coals of consciousness which have not been stirred for a long time.

In the book "*Sri Aurobindo, The Adventure of Consciousness*"[31], the author describes the idea of consciousness as "not something to be found ready-made, but something to be kindled like a fire". He goes on to say:

---

[31] Satprem, *Sri Aurobindo: or The Adventure of Consciousness* (New York: Institute For Evolutionary Research, 1984), p. 39.

*Who would not bear witness to this pure enthusiasm, this inexplicable nostalgia of this place that exists within us. Gradually (however) the mind lays hold of this force as it does of everything, covers it up with big idealizing words, and sets it into a work, a profession, a church. Or the vital being seizes upon it and daubs it with more or less noble sentiments when it does not use it for some adventure or for domination, conquest, or possession. The seeker who has silenced his mind and can no longer be trapped by ideas, who has calmed his emotional nature and is not swept away at every moment in the great wastage of feelings and desires, rediscovers in this clarification of his nature, like a new state of youth, a new free surge internally. As his concentration grows stronger through active meditation, by his aspiration, his need, he will feel that this surge inside him begins to live . . . this force in him has movement, a mass, varying intensities, and it rises and descends with him, in him, as if it were not steady...*[32]

There is something within us that if we concentrate upon it is like a ray of sun that

---

[32] Ibid., p. 60.

shines through glass and causes a fire. It is as if the ray of sun is there within. If you concentrate, you can cause the "fire" and feel it charging and moving inside you.

Have you ever felt that you could contact a "force" within you that you couldn't describe? When you concentrated upon it, called upon it, prayed to it, asked for it, you could feel it ignite like a flame and you knew it had a life. Could you then feel it cool down and get quiet until you gave it your attention once more?

Previously, I indicated that during much of our lives consciousness "leaks in". This might occur as you are walking alone in a natural setting, while you are listening to music, or when you find yourself in love. It may be an exquisite moment looking at the stars or a perfect shot in your golf game. Something special happens within — something really happens within — consciousness has leaked in.

Why does this occur? Because in that split second, everything harmonizes — mind, body, emotions, and environment come together. When it happens, you are caught by the power of it. Your awareness of what has always been there increases and that, in turn, intensifies your demand that it be ever-present. In such moments, the veil is split for a second. The shroud is lifted for a second; the light ray penetrates through; the sun fires the flame. We are enflamed and we respond to it.

> "This force [in you] has movement, a mass, varying intensities. It rises and descends within as if it were not steady, much like the shifting of a living substance. These inner movements can even gather a strength that is sufficiently great to enter the body, when the force descends, or to straighten it up and draw it back when it rises."[33]

I am very aware when it enters me; it gives me a kind of energy far beyond human energy. That is why I feel a terrible lack when it goes away.

> "It is not only an impersonal force, but a presence, a being in our depths as though we had a support there, something that gives us a solidity, almost a backbone, and a quiet outlook on the world."[34]

---

[33] Ibid., p. 61.

[34] Ibid., p. 60-61.

The word "Quiet", here, does not mean that you are not thinking or doing or experiencing. "Quiet" means that the inner "you" is sustained within.

> *"One is invulnerable and no longer alone. It becomes the same thing everywhere in all beings and all things. We experience that we are exactly alike without a wall. We feel as if we have touched the fundamental reality of our being our self, truly our self, in the true center, warmth and being, the consciousness force."*[35]

These quotations from Aurobindo are the best description I have ever read of my experience with this energy, this consciousness. It is because of its power that we, in our hunger, desire to tap into it, to continually aspire towards it.

Aurobindo has also spoken of the process of refining this consciousness force within us. "Refining" tends to be a word we want to resist. We prefer to consider that anything that is natural will be there, and participation or refinement is not necessary. I have heard that

---

[35] Ibid., p. 61.

concept for years. People say, "If I've got it, why must I do anything about it?"

Aurobindo says:

> *The task of the apprentice yogi will be to become conscious in every way at all the levels of his being and all the stages of universal existence, not only mentally.*[36]

Consider this: when you look through yourself, are you aware of your fortes? The areas where you are competent? Incompetent? Ask yourself whether you are primarily a mental being? Is that how you relate to life? Do you consider yourself a "heart" being? Do you consider yourself a solar plexus being? Do you find that some days or moments, you are all head, all heart, all solar plexus, all sex? Because of that, do you feel confused? Do you feel as if you are jumping around from one to the other and maybe even a bit schizophrenic because you cannot hold it all together?

My interpretation is that you are being given opportunities to move through awareness of

---

[36] Ibid., p. 53.

your whole being. So Aurobindo is stating that our part is to become conscious in every way.

At times I have felt narcissistic: all I did during this period of intense self-observation was to think upon me, and this was of concern. I became aware of how much I had been thinking only of me all my life. These periods of intense self-scrutiny allowed me to begin moving away from the self-centeredness. Paradoxically, the only way to move away from self-centeredness is by studying the self more intensely. It does not happen through avoidance and resistance but through exposure and acceptance. We must start where we are, love ourselves there, and consciousness itself can then fire. These are very important words.

Aurobindo goes on to say, "One becomes... conscious in himself and others and in things, in waking and in sleep."[37]

Sometimes you may begin to have psychic awareness which you tune into. People tell me of their suddenly having weird thoughts, and I experienced the same. I would go into stores,

---

[37] Ibid.

look at people and pick up on their fears, sadness, depression. I had never experienced that before. I doubted myself and wondered if I was projecting myself upon others. Then, as I began to trust myself, I realized I had become so intuitive and psychic that I was picking up the energy and thoughts of others.

You can expect to become much more wide open and that will produce fear, naturally. But one learns to be more open and comfortable with it.

Aurobindo completes this thought by stating that one's goal, the goal of a yogi, is to be fully conscious in life and then one can be conscious in death. He continues,

> *"First we see the general confusion in which we live slowly settling down."* [38]

You begin to become aware of this consciousness, you begin to increase your capacity to see how really "weird" you have been.

---

[38] Ibid., p. 53.

For example, I could not believe how much anger was in me. I could not believe that I used my anger to get and keep me going. I could not believe that was my composition and incentive. I could not believe how I grind mentally on the material of my life.

Aurobindo continues:

> *The stages of our being become distinguished more and more clearly, as though we were made of a certain number, of fragments, each with its individual personality and a distinct center. There is not a single movement of our being, no matter what level, not an emotion, a desire, a twinkling of an eye which is not immediately shaped by the mind and covered by a coating of thought. We mentalize everything. The seeker who has silenced his mind begins to distinguish all these states and their naked reality without their mental veneer.*[39]

I had an experience with that today. I was watering a plant and felt a sense of oneness. I heard doubt in my mind, expressed by the thought, "I think you are bored." I had to look

---

[39] Ibid., p. 53-54.

at the thought, "I think you are bored" and say, "Oh, cut it out — that is absurd. Go bother somebody else."

When these subtleties come into our system, there is a psychotherapeutic process which encourages that we dialogue with them, communicate with them, throw a pillow at them, discuss them, or write them in a soul journal. I did that practice for years, and it really worked; but now it is time to be done. Now, I look and observe and watch it die without attachment.

Aurobindo has stated elsewhere that most thought stuff comes from the outside. It is mesmeric conditioning[40] and does not come from the personality.

> *"A seeker of silence is willing to distinguish all these states in their naked reality without mental veneer."*[41]

---

[40] [Mesmeric conditioning is an unconscious, hypnotic conditioning from our culture that we accept without questioning.] ed. Coy F. Cross II

[41] Ibid., p. 54.

The boring thought was a moment of naked reality, and in a period of ten hours that thought was the only one that could have caught me, pulled me down, or done me in.

*"You feel at the various levels of your being, certain points of concentration, like a knot of force, each with its particular vibratory quality and special frequency."* [42]

A knot of force, to use Aurobindo's term, is a place where you can feel a lot of energy centered, maybe even stuck or locked. It draws your attention. All of a sudden you find yourself drawn to a part of your body or you find yourself drawn to a thought or drawn to a situation — that is a knot of force. It is sitting there wanting to be broken up by your giving it attention and concentration.

Aurobindo goes on to explain:

*We have all experienced at least once in our lives, different vibrations which seem to radiate from diverse levels of our being, the experience of more heavy vibrations of anger or fear,*

---

[42] Ibid.

*desire, sympathy. All these pulsate at different levels with different intensities. There is the whole gamut of vibratory nodules or centers of consciousness. These centers are not situated in our physical body but in another dimension, though their concentration at certain moments may become so intense that there is the acute sensation of a physical localization.*[43]

To summarize, we are a consciousness force, every one of us, all of every one of us. That consciousness force is shrouded. The way to reconnect with that force is through the refinement and clarification of a subtle sensitivity to the physical, mental, emotional and environmental status of each of us.

Only as we become intensely aware can we take away the power from it. Then it cannot block us from being connected with this power within that continually wants to radiate outward through us. That is what we are attempting to do.

---

[43] Ibid., p. 55.

*TOOLS FOR DEVELOPING CONSCIOUSNESS*

Much of this material comes from studies of the Eastern Orthodox Church fathers who separated themselves from the Roman Catholic Church early after Jesus died and carved the schism that occurred at the time of the Council of Nicea.

The group called Gnostics developed a special, internal religious experience that moved away from the larger, more social, dogmatic Roman Catholic direction of the church. The Gnostics taught that we must first follow Jesus' teaching "to love the Lord, your God, with all your mind and all your heart and all your soul."

They are specific in how to do this: You think about God all the time, if possible. The *"Philokalia"*[44] explains, "A man stands at prayer and raising his hands, his eyes and his mind to heaven, keeps in mind divine thought, imagines celestial blessings, hierarchies of angels, and dwellings of the saints, assembles briefly in his

---

[44] E. Kadloubovsky and G.E.H. Palmer, trans, *Writings from the Philokalia on Prayer of the Heart* (London: Faber and Faber Limited, 1951), p. 153.

mind all that he has learned from Holy Scriptures and ponders over all this while at prayer."

*CONSCIOUS THOUGHT TOWARDS GOD*

The foregoing quotation suggests this ongoing prayer begins at times of active prayer.

In active prayer, one gradually gathers his whole mind into this attitude and gradually prayer becomes one's life. All the teachers state that one's whole mind must be consciously praying without distraction. Such activity is extremely difficult.

If you were at a monastic class in 200 to 300 A.D., your first lesson would instruct you that all times, starting now, your goal would be to have your mind centered only upon thoughts about God. That is how you would be expected to conduct your daily life.

I have done this activity full time, and it has worked powerfully. This teaching is similar to the Unity teaching of affirmation.

I practice this activity when I am alone with myself driving. I do it when I wake in the morning and the last thing as I go to sleep at night. I do it when I am in the kitchen preparing food. When I garden, this is what I seek to do. I do it by watching my thought and continually encouraging it to be God-oriented.

As you read this, you must realize that a seed is being sown for you to consider. What you do with it, if you ever do anything with it, will be your own experience.

First you will have to discover what a God thought is.

Nobody knows what a God thought is, but there is something that helps — you find it is a constant pushing inside which says, "That doesn't fit and not that, and not that, and not that". It pushes and grows and pushes and grows.

It is terribly exciting to watch it work. As it, works, you find that you are refining thoughts, emotions, body and lifestyles.

There was something inside me that knew I no longer wanted to run down a one-way mental track to engage in some analytical spiel. The minute I made the decision to develop the consciousness force, something inside me knew that my attention must be internal to succeed.

Another more common practice is to carry a mantra in the mind all the time. For instance, carry the mantra, "There is only one presence and one power in the universe, God". Roman Catholics use the Jesus prayer, "Lord Jesus Christ, have mercy upon me." The fascinating thing is that it matters little what is said if the intention is "Godly".

It is like a well-trained baseball player in the outfield — it doesn't matter whether the baseball field is created to make money, to win fame, to advertise Jockey shorts. When the ball is hit the player feels where the ball is going and his thoughts move with it.

That is what the psycho cybernetics system meant: something knows, and when triggered, it moves. That is also true of you. Once the intention of your being has committed to this then only establishing a consistent, even prayer matters. The rest works on its own.

Notice how different this practice is from how we usually spend our lives. Most of our lives, we only do this kind of participating when we are in trouble. Many of us go to God when we have been kicked in the rear. When I started my ministry, I used to say, "What a shame that we don't communicate with God all the time rather than when it is just a little bit too late".

It's clear that my whole life has led me to spend my full time communicating with God at least as I have come to understand what it is to communicate with God. Communicating with God becomes a way of life, a refinement process that goes on inside all the time.

## TRANSITION

Everything has a stage which leads to another stage, because the nature of anything is to reveal its weaknesses with use.

Let's pretend that a group of people sat around and did this practice for a long time. I have practiced with the people closest to me. One friend and I would get together and we would discuss how this practice was going and what was happening within us. I think this may be what happened to these early Christian monastics as well. They discovered some problems in the discipline.

One problem is that this practice limits the awareness available to you; it is a very mental procedure. The limitation is that you are defining what God thoughts are, trying to keep your mind narrowed into that range, and putting a lot of conscious pressure on yourself. It is tiring, flattening, and a deadening experience. It can take you into the dark night of the soul quickly, however, because you begin to eliminate so much of the natural "you" for the sake of the commitment. You don't want to give yourself away to this thought or that thought. You become intensely aware that your energy can no longer go outside; it can only go inside.

Another part of this stage is recorded in the book, *"The Way of the Pilgrim"*.[45] It is the story of a peasant who started doing this practice. After doing this practice for a week, he returned to his priest guide and asked why he had become so aware of who he was, and why he was so overwhelmed with the ugly nature of his true thoughts.

During this practice, you do become aware of your true thoughts, all of them. It is difficult to

---

[45] R.M. French, trans, *The Way of the Pilgrim* and *The Pilgrim Continues His Way* (San Francisco: Harper Collins, Publishers, 1965).

see who you really are, how you function, but knowing that will lead you on.

I had the most beautiful moment one day as I was feeding some begonia plants. My mind said, "My God, what an exciting trip this has been!" There are tears in me wanting to tell you it has been an exciting and wonderful journey as well as a frightening and horrible journey.

*ELIMINATION OF THAT WHICH DOES NOT FIT*

Another prayer practice, often done concurrently with keeping one's attention on God is called "denial".

Human beings have created the denial just as they have created the church. I would assume that denial was created because people could not handle fear. By using a denial they tell the fear to go away.

I did a lot of this early in my life. I would use phrases like, "I will not give you power. The Christ within me is greater than anything that is in the world". That is a great Unity statement.

In the Hindu tradition, this practice is called "Neti Neti", which is Sanskrit for "not this and not that". God is not this and God is not that.

It is a way of weaning, a way of cleansing, a way of screening, a way of discriminating and a way of taking care of that which concerns the person. By doing this, you are trying to take life's fear and confusion and translate it into God and light.

The denial may be done at the same time as thinking about God, as a parallel activity. To exemplify this, let's imagine that you have a fear that somebody is more powerful than you, or that they are taking energy from you. You realize that you cannot be possessed by them anymore. They cannot be that big in your mind and thought. Denial would be to say within, "You don't fit in me anymore; I want you to go".

Within a second, of course, you find they are back in your mind; you are thinking about the issue, trying to figure it out or explain it away. Then you have to remind yourself again and say, "Listen, I don't want you in my 'space' anymore. I free you to go". You may get two seconds without it this time and there it is again. So you say: "There is a power within me that is dominant and powerful. It is the Christ within me and personality does not reign in my mind, my life and my affairs."

Remember, we may even experience this with somebody whom we admire, whom we want to follow, whom we think has all the answers. Yet, even in love you finally have to do this with everybody — your greatest love and your greatest hate — become detached. That is denial.

To review, realizing there are thoughts and feelings going on inside you that you don't want there, you say, "I don't want you around anymore". You say that inside you; that's all. You do it for everything and anything. It could be realizing that you are dominated by sexual desire, natural desire, or food desire. But remember, this desire to deny must come from inside you or it won't work.

I am not saying to you that you should not be dominated by a person or a desire, rather something will move inside you and it is that aspiration, the consciousness force, saying, "Hey, I don't know whether I want that going on in me anymore". And the denial goes to work saying, "I don't want to have you have so much power over me". It may be a recognition that you are too attached to material things. It may be a realization that all your life you have "gone for it", and you really bought into creating your own reality, and then you found you are possessed by it. As these realizations come along, you say, "I don't want to have that going on anymore. I am the master in here".

This is not repression. The difference between repression and denial is this. Repression is not allowing yourself to see what it is that has hold of you because you are afraid of it.

If you keep letting a thing come to the surface and say within yourself, "I don't need to let you dominate me anymore", then you are not repressing.

If you keep on loving yourself then you do not have to repress; you know there is nothing that can beat you. When an issue comes to the surface, and you know that you don't want it there anymore, don't attack it. Love yourself for its existence in you. Allow it to be there in you and in the allowing you can let it go.

An example of this is in our attitude towards food. So many people get so upset and confused about their eating. They deny that food has any power in their life, but that does not work. The reason it doesn't work is because they don't love the need within them that wants fulfillment which food provides.

If they keep on loving the need within themselves, then gradually it will alter in form and the true need will reveal itself at a deeper level. Always the true need within is for a greater realization of God.

### THE MENTAL QUIETING — ANOTHER TRANSITION

After you have done these two exercises for a period of time, you may begin to become such a student of the mind that you can look at your mind's little thoughts and accept them all as unimportant. As you give less and less power and energy to those thoughts, you are moving along quickly because you are getting close to the ability to "kiss the mind good-bye". Saying good-bye to your mind is a frightening experience.

We all recognize, for instance, that if our minds were to go entirely, we could not continue our work. Having the mind go means that it gets so quiet it does not function as prominently anymore. When your mind moves into that state, and these processes will help it happen, you can experience a lot of the feelings of the dark night of the soul.

If you wish to study more of this, read any of

Rajneesh's[46] writings, especially, *"The Mustard Seed".*[47]

Rajneesh will tell you it is essential that the mind become still. Why? Because the mind is your tool for relating to the world. It has done all the teaching of you, all the conditioning. It carries the beliefs. It has all the answers, all the analyses. It has been trained as a problem-solving tool.

But once you start observing the mind, you realize that the mind is a fool's tool. You realize that its nature is to attend to anything that is an issue or a problem. It will go to uncanny extremes to make life appear as if it were real. It will go down the longest corridors to make something out of nothing. It will even convince itself that it has feelings, that it has a body, that

---

[46] Chandra Mohan Jain, 11 December 1931 – 19 January 1990 was also known as Acharya Rajneesh from the 1960s onwards, as Bhagwan Shree Rajneesh, during the 1970s and 1980s, and as Osho from 1989; he was an Indian mystic, guru, and spiritual teacher.

[47] Bhagwan Shree Rajneesh, *The Mustard Seed: Discourses on the Sayings of Jesus Taken from the Gospel According to Thomas* (New York: Harper Collins, Publishers, 1978).

it has friends, and that it is here to do something that has meaning.

Then you realize that if there were some way to get out of your mind, then you would have the secret. The greatest fear in the world is to lose your mind, right? Isn't that what the psychiatrist says, "My God, she has lost her mind. He went out of his head."?

If we really understood that, we might have a different attitude about our mental institutions. Then they might be filled with our spiritual leaders. Be careful, the mind's role is to clarify. It is not bad — it has a role. But letting its natural role dominate you and keep you from greater depth is frustrating and limiting, and denies the potential for expansion and creativity.

In the chapter entitled the "*Silent Mind*"[48], Aurobindo states, "Once we have this realization that the mind is like fool's gold, the mind is the illusion, we are in quest for another country, but it would be well to say, between the one we leave behind and the one which is

------

[48] Satprem, *The Adventures of Consciousness*, p. 36.

not yet found there is a fairly painful no-man's
land."

We are beginning to get leaders who are writing
books to help guide people through no-man's
land. Aurobindo states:

> *This is a period of trial, more or less long,*
> *according to our determination. But at all times*
> *we know from the Asiatic, Egyptian*
> *initiations to the quest of the Holy Grail, the*
> *story of man's assent has been attended by*
> *trials. Early in our history they were romantic,*
> *now they are mystical. The main ordeal of this*
> *transition is the inner void. After having lived*
> *in a mental feverishness, one finds oneself*
> *suddenly like a convalescent.*[49]

Often, I would experience this while driving.
Suddenly, I would be shocked to find that
nothing was going on in my mind; there were
no thoughts. I would go scouring around inside
my "wonderful" mind. Then I thought, I must
be burnt out. I wasn't burnt out; I was just in
transition. My mind is not gone. It will never

---

[49] Ibid., p. 36.

go. When this void happens, I must be patient. The worst fear is that this state will never end.

Aurobindo suggests:

> *One finds himself a bit like a convalescent, a bit lost with strange humming in the head—as though this world were terribly noisy, tiring— and the acute sensibility which gives the impression of being knocked about everywhere against opaque and aggressive men, heavy objects, food or events. This is a sure sign of the beginning of interiorization (not craziness). However, if one tries to descend consciously inside by meditating, one finds a similar void, a sort of dark well or an amorphous neutrality. If one persists in descending, one glides suddenly into sleep for two seconds, ten seconds, two minutes longer, in fact, not an ordinary sleep. We have only passed into another consciousness, but there is no link yet between the two, and one comes out of it not more advanced, apparently, than one had entered. There is nothing outside and there is nothing within either. And it is here that we must be very careful when demolishing our outer mental construction, not to become enclosed again in a false profundity under another construction,*

*absurd illusion. We must go farther to the very end whatever it may cost.* [50]

This is the stilling of the mind, and it comes because you have recognized that the "outer" does not serve anymore, and the natural result is that the mind quiets down.

I assure you that the mind does not stop; the mind cannot stop. If you are sitting inside and nothing is going on, it means that the mind is still going on, but the mirror is so clear that it seems absolutely still. And it is waiting for deeper subtleties of thought.

Aurobindo:

*Here indeed is the trial. The seeker must understand that he is being born to another Life, that his new eyes, new senses are not yet born, like those of the newborn child who are lights in the world. This is a passage.* [51]

Mental quiet is a preface to being still. The idea is that you build a quiet place inside that allows

---

[50] Ibid., p. 37.

[51] Ibid.

the mind to do whatever it wants but cannot disturb the one who sits inside. You cannot shut off the mind, the mind won't shut off, but you can slow the mind down.

Being in a class speeds up your mind; talking speeds up your mind; improper food speeds up your mind; sports speed up your mind. Your whole life must become supportive of this quieting. This process of quieting the mind is an intermediary stage between the first two prayer practices and the next. It is a growing awareness to be understood and supported.

### PRACTICING THE PRESENCE

Next, we can participate in 'Practicing the Presence'. Thinking about God is a mental activity. Denial is a mental activity. Quieting the mind is the beginning of interiorizing the self. It is also the beginning of becoming more grounded, not needing to get away from yourself so that you can stand being in you, right here with whatever is going on and loving yourself as you are. As you are moving through that, Practicing the Presence becomes a valuable process.

In this prayer, you move from putting your attention mentally on God to bringing your focus down into your heart and dwelling on God. You can do it right this minute by placing your awareness in your heart and keeping it there.

The Jesus Prayer is "Lord Jesus Christ, Son of God, have mercy on me, for I am a sinner." If you keep yourself there with a slight mantra going, like I AM, or the Jesus Prayer, you can begin to feel a powerful inner rhythm and movement stirring. You have tapped into the consciousness force.

Then you begin to affect the energy in your body. Through your attention, you ignite the fire and allow this energy to release itself and expand.

The first and second stages are essential cleansing stages and the third stage is an awareness stage. This one, Practicing the Presence, is where you begin to become a catalytic agent in your own process of releasing this energy.

We all do this occasionally, in other areas. You want to paint a picture. To do that, you give your focus to it. In this case, we really give focus to our own self, our own life energy. That is the only difference.

Something wonderful happens once you start Practicing the Presence. The practice is as simple as I have described and yet subtle and individual in its effects. It leads to a great deal of freedom and finally to the fourth stage of prayer, grace.

Before explaining grace, I would like to share some of the results of practicing the Presence. They have been soul-satisfying, uplifting, and sustaining.

Realize that I had used the first two prayer practices most of my life, from the time I was ten. At ten, I also started meditating. It wasn't until 1977 that I started practicing constant meditation which is what I consider Practicing the Presence to be.

After three years of such practice, I had a profound mystical experience. I was awakened in the middle of the night and "sitting" right in front of my breast was a Germanic cross. It was shimmering in luminous metallic color. Gradually, it moved very, very slowly and implanted itself through my chest about an eighth of an inch beneath my breastbone. When I awoke that morning I could feel the huge force, all around me. I was wrapped in love, and I knew it. Within an hour, if went away but it left me with a warmth in my chest that was there all the time for about five days. Every time I wanted to I could feel this presence in my chest. It felt like being in love physically and whenever I am in love physically my whole body experiences it, a marvelous sensation. When it stopped, I felt very sad; but I knew, as you know, that when a thing is done, it is done.

In fact, as it left me, it told me it had other work to do.

## GRACE

All during that year, I had increasing experiences with this huge energy field coming into me and I began to have a glimpse of the final stage of participation — grace.

Grace is a gift of God. It is always talked about in this way, biblically and by spiritual teachers. Grace is that element I was referring to at the start of this section, when I said that each of us has within us an inner splendor which is usually shrouded.

One first gets a sense of grace in the fleeting wisp, the "leak" referred to in the first section

— that flash which wings through you. Once experienced, you begin your mission, and your goal is to be there all the time. You learn so much on the way, and one of the last things you learn is to stop even asking to be constantly one with God. Give up even your desire for God. Isn't it funny that you start this journey desiring to be one with God and then you learn that you have to give up your desires, you have to give up everything, and the last one is even asking to be one with God?

Grace feels like experiencing that the limits of gravity are cut. You are no longer earthbound. You are totally supported and taken care of and loved. You are totally vulnerable and yet totally incapable of being harmed. You have to be both at the same time, when you are in grace.

There is a beautiful picture done by Dali[52], a picture of only the hands of God reaching down and lifting up two very small people, carrying and caring for them. That is how you

---

[52] Salvador Felipe Jacinto Dali I Domenech was born 1904 in Figueres, Spain. He helped lead the artistic Surrealist Movement and his courageous explorations and symbolic complexity set a standard for twentieth century art.

feel when you are in grace — as if some other force comes in and takes you over and carries you for a while.

The sad thing always is that you feel dropped; but even when that comes, you know it is all right.

I often experience the fullness of grace and the feeling of "all is well". In fact, I nearly always feel "'all is well", regardless of the external situations. But sometimes you can feel grace carry you, lift you, support you, and take care of you for an extended period of time.

The last stage in terms of participation is you do not have to participate. At the point of grace, life becomes a dance.

# 6: CAROL RUTH KNOX'S PROCESS CHART

This diagram will assist in explaining the different layers as Carol Ruth perceived them in a person's growth and development. It gives a "feeling" for levels of soul evolution in what appears to be three stages.

There have, no doubt, been earlier ones that no longer can be seen as they have been lopped off in the evolutionary process. She had not experienced levels beyond the mystical, but sensed they were possible. Words defining each stage are listed parallel to each other.

Be careful of your individual response to the words as they have deeper and more complex meanings than their simple usage often denotes.

*(The chart is on the next two pages)*

| Process Chart | | |
|---|---|---|
| **Traditional (Victim)** | **First closet (Birth canal)** | **Metaphysical (Victor)** |
| Unconscious | | Conscious |
| Waiting | | Doing/having |
| Physical | | Emotional |
| Instinctual | | Mental |
| 1st chakra | | 2nd and 3rd chakra |
| No ego | | Strong ego |
| Has no effect | Death of dependent Self | Karmic law |
| No choice | | Choice |
| No will | | Will |
| No control | | Control/manipulation |
| Begging | | Affirmation/denial |
| Irresponsibility | | Responsibility |

| Process Chart | |
| --- | --- |
| **Second closet (Birth canal)** | **Mystical (Vehicle)** |
| | Consciously not conscious |
| | Being |
| | Spiritual |
| | Intuitive |
| 4th chakra | 5th through 7th chakra |
| | Egoless |
| Dark Night of the soul | Beyond karmic |
| | Freedom from choice |
| Death of self | Divine will |
| | Give up control |
| | Ongoing prayer (grace) |
| | Available to respond |

# 7: LIVING THE SPIRITUAL LIFE

## *REVIEW*

Within us is an aspiring quality working, moving, pushing and reaching. Whenever anything is completed in the Universe, there is an aspiration to accomplish, to live out something new, different. That aspiration, that quality, is the part of us that longs to feel unity and oneness with something essential.

There is definitely a process for moving toward this "Oneness". I have described it in the following way: first, we are unconscious, then a force starts pushing us into becoming more conscious; this moves us into a conscious realm of seeking, aiming and asserting. While in this conscious realm, that same force begins to penetrate into the conscious pushing us again into a new space. Once this occurs, we move into a period of limbo, of feeling lost. This is the "dark night of the soul". After adjusting to this stage, we enter a state of beingness where we become comfortable with being "created through". At this

135

point, our personality gets out of the way; we become "vessels," no longer concerned with questions like "Who am I?" and "Where am I going?" We become Essence; we become Life itself.

To move through the difficulty and discomfort of these changes, one must have courage, be willing to participate, and develop trust.

The courage required is not an overcoming courage; it is the courage to be, to hold onto the ground of one's being. Participation may sound strange — why would a person have to participate in something that is natural, evolutionary? Yet, conscious participation is necessary to support the internal movement, to break the beliefs, to release the fears, thereby encouraging the process as it occurs.

Trust means that everything is always in Divine Order. That quality of trust is recognizably elaborate and huge in scope. The deepest trust is the appreciation that everybody, everything, every organization has its special process. No one can put that process in stone; it cannot be monumentalized; it can only be experienced and lived out. One's capacity for trusting all as a part of God includes mistakes, traumas, tragedies, joys, love, fear. All is in Divine Order. Nothing is out of order. When that is grasped, the belief is full and integrated.

The last chapter presented how one might actually participate. Active participation allows for all life parts to become refined and brought into order, including one's relationship to the environment, to other people, to economics, to self.

All of that must be refined, not because somebody outside is requesting or demanding it, but because something inside begins to see clearly that refining will release the inner splendor.

Then the aspiring quality is released by recognizing there is a flame within each person. The role of the participant is to become his own catalytic agent for triggering this inner flame.

Procedures to assist in being this catalyst are: thinking about God (affirmation), letting go of that which no longer fits (denial), and quieting the mind in order to become still inside.

A quiet mind is not one that stops, but rather one that is quiet internally no matter where it is; a quiet mind is detached, no longer involved.

Developing a quiet mind often leads to a sense of the dark night of the soul, since detachment gives a feeling of tremendous distance and inability to be part of the external world. Quieting the mind and a willingness to experience the dark night of the soul leads to acceptance of being in a "state of being". All of this takes time and patience.

Practicing the Presence is another early Christian practice, in which the attention is moved from the head or intellect into the heart. This step leads to expansion and a feeling of interior grace, an ever-present feeling that the Power Itself can come into and carry you. You no longer are seeking and aspiring in one direction, the Power "comes down" and begins to be a part of your life without your having to consciously participate.

The analogy was made to a dancer or an artist setting out, learning to perform, being caught in self, then being released from that and gaining a feeling of pure freedom where the music, the art, takes over. That also happens in the spiritual life, except, instead of doing a dance for the public or giving a speech for others, the life is the doing.

## PHILOSOPHY FOR LIVING/ DOING THE SPIRITUAL LIFE

My hope is that I have prepared you to recognize a very important effect: that if you make this kind of major transformation, your life becomes your own; your life energy becomes an orb in which you sit. The externals no longer tell you what to do; the inner life dictates the direction.

When we are born, we are programmed, conditioned, according to the information that life projects at us. That information is imprinted upon our brains as neuron patterns. Without our knowing it, we are taught how to be, think, and react. We generally live our lives repeating that programming, projecting it back on whatever we see or do. There is nothing wrong with this — most people live their entire lives this way.

However, once one moves through the stages of being conscious and the dark night into a state of being, a dramatic occurrence takes place. There is a tendency for society and organizations to not want this to happen because once it does the individual becomes his own person and is unable to be controlled.

The dramatic occurrence is that instead of being at "effect," the person is at "cause". All actions come through you not because of previous programming, but because the Life Energy and Spirit provide the direction. At this stage, all action manifests, not because the person is responding to previous programming or conditioning, but because the Energy Force is now expressing through the person. The results may be the same, but the impetus is entirely different.

The theme for this section, then is, "living the Spiritual Life in the world," and the checkout system for living this way is, "Is this action coming from within me or is it programmed externally?" Coming from within does not mean from the ego, from programming or from the personality. It means coming through the Spirit within directly into the person.

Many people in the conscious stage get excited about creating. They say, "I am going to create my own reality." It is an ego-filled time to see yourself building things, creating something out of nothing. What are you actually creating? You are actually creating your own conditionings, which is actually re-presenting old information rather than creating new. It is actually a state of re-creating.

A specific example might be that all your life you have seen that successful people drive Mercedes, so when you get the feeling of your own power, you assert, "I want to create a Mercedes." Or, all your life you have been programmed to want a blond, cool, lean, sensual woman. If you go into a treasure-mapping class, you place a picture of a Mercedes and this type of woman in the treasure map. Maybe, for you, it is a college education, going up the ladder of success to become vice president, or selling more homes as a realtor. In doing that thinking or treasure mapping, you believe you are "creating". Then when you manifest these things you say, "God is working for me. Look what I manifested."

Another way this works might be if you were to experience an illness. In this instance, you would program into your mind that you want to cure that illness based upon the belief that a healthy body would not have illness. In each of the preceding cases, the person involved does not realize that what they are really doing is re-creating a former programming. This is not the true creativity of letting Spirit move through to create as it would, because when Spirit moves through the individual, the person truly does not have a clear sense of what is going to be formed until it arrives.

This is a very important point. Spirit creates as senses, not pre-programmed structures. There are not words, there are no pictures. There is a sense. Sense could be defined as "light, intuition, perception, insight, flash." It does not come as gut feelings. When asked how they know something is right, many people say, "My gut tells me."

Now, what the gut tells you may be right in terms of an emotional response. But when you are moving from a point of Being, Spirit awareness does not come through the gut; it does not come through the head; it comes through sensing and intuition which is a different language system.

Saying I want this and this and this is not the level of functioning I am striving to clarify in this presentation. Working at this level of purity means you keep letting yourself be led: like a stream that is meandering — you let yourself go to each place to which you are taken. Then when you see whatever is to become a part of the life, it is recognized and becomes incorporated.

When I bought the furniture for my home eight years ago, I went to a furniture store and the sales people would ask, "What do you want, lady?" I would say, "Just show me what you have, and when I see it, I'll know it." Now they didn't appear to like that at all because I slowed them down immensely.

During this summer, as I have looked for property, what was moving inside was that when I found the place, I would feel it and I would feel "the dirt wrap up around me." I would know. So although I have been embarrassed that I didn't find what I said I thought I was going for, the truth is that the Spirit is leading every act. This is not because I am rationalizing or manipulating myself, but because that is the way it is working.

"Creating your own reality" and "Living from being" are entirely different. Living from being, you are "at instantaneous cause". You may still go about planning your future. You may make investments, decide to get married, buy a house. You may do all kinds of things, but you do them with an understanding that even the fantasies, even the mental manipulations, are the instant activity of the guidance system that is taking you every step of the way.

## RELATIONSHIPS

My primary intent in this chapter is action — doing the Spiritual Life. Action is very important. In fact, as I now see it, if you want to know what a person is, watch what they do!

But don't laugh at them because earlier they had said that they were going to do something else. Just realize that what they had said they were going to do is not what they did — they did what they did. Incidentally, we are always farther ahead of ourselves, mentally and emotionally, than we are with our actions. We call each other hypocrites because our head and our hearts lead us — they may be a year, or two years or five years ahead of their action in the world. Think about that with your children, yourselves, and your mates. It will free you and them from guilt.

This section will be devoted to "action with regard to relationships" as we live the Spiritual life in the world. It will include relationship to oneself, relationship to others, relationship to the earth, relationship to work and economy, and relationship to change, death and life. We tend to think there is only one kind of relationship when we use the word. Most people talk only about human relationships, and human relationships are a large part of our lives. Clearly, if you cannot make it with your fellow beings, then you have deep, inner problems.

Yet, relationship means, as well, how a person connects with everything that goes on around them. Our whole life is about relationships. What guideline, what standard for relating to the earth, the physical body and the material substances shall be used?

Now that the Spiritual path has led to a state of "being", now that we are communicating from Spirit within, how do we bring that through; what are the guidelines for all relationships?

How we connect with what is outside begins with the individual. What is outside is not only material things: your body is outside; your mind is outside; your emotions are outside, as well as all else. In terms of my Essence and my Core, (which is a peaceful flowing river, at Oneness always, unchanging) how am I going to bring that through, to work with the issues that are my life?

One other thought to consider with regard to relationships is separation — the necessary separation from relationships at times, as we seek to become closer to our Spiritual Self. Relating can only be as effective as we have the courage to be separate, to separate from all that is going on, and thereby sustain ourselves.

There is a lot of fear when someone says, "I am going away to be alone, to be still." If our mate says I need to get away and be by myself, we think they don't like us anymore. If our children withdraw for two or three days we wonder what's wrong with them. Cindy, my dog, every so often, has a period where she goes away. Her eyes get kind-of weird looking and she becomes temperamental and very standoffish. That is the natural system, essentially, which has to go away. It goes away not only to nourish, but also to build energy, so that it can come back again.

We are always going away to come back, and very few of us have permission to do that. Such ebb and flow can actually create psychological warfare within and with others. Since we don't feel good about withdrawing, escaping, the unclear need left unfulfilled can cause paranoia, schizophrenia. Withdrawal and escape are seen as diseases in our society. But, they are not diseases; they are a part of our system, and only if we are going to be afraid of them can they make us ill.

There is a natural tendency to go away. Sometimes we do it as a major statement about our life. Many divorces are statements saying, I have to go away for a while, and I didn't know how to do it with you, so I am going away permanently.

The Bible teaches that not until one loses himself will he find himself. Many of Jesus' teachings, like that in the Prodigal Son, incorporate the idea of going away and coming back.

Chardin[53] states that when cell structures come together to form a larger structure, they consolidate into a little area that is too compacted.

---

[53] Pierre Teilhard de Chardin.

At this point, one little cell breaks away and leaves the group. It goes away to rebuild itself, to restore itself, and then it returns — it always returns.

Few of us have been taught that if you go away or withdraw, you always return. Instead, we are taught that withdrawal is dangerous.

The Spiritual teaching offers a deep reflection: if you withdraw, love yourself.

You see, if you can go away and feel good about it, then restoration occurs, but if you go away and feel bad about it, you will not restore, for you will spend all your time beating yourself because you should be back and involved. Think about how much you do this.

If one goes away in self-love, the being restores and always returns.

In the cell example, the cell returns by reinserting itself in the already over-pressurized cell casing — like the straw that breaks the camel's back, it is the last little bit of pressure which causes the old form to expand into the next creation in the Universal order of things (another peduncle). If this did not happen, the next form could not come into existence.

### RELATIONSHIP TO ONE'S SELF

The preceding material has been provided to let you see how necessary it is to first take care of yourself, if you would live the Spiritual Life in the world. I am asking you to take the threat away from yourself, and to help others do the same.

First, we must take care of ourselves, if your relationship with yourself is to take care of everybody else first, then you will finally damage you so that you will have nothing left to give.

And we have a society that is still built upon "give to others, do for others, take care of everybody else first." We are frightened to say, "No." This means that if your world is crumbling, your mate is dying, your children are running crazy, even then, your self must be built, restored.

So, the first relationship is the relationship to one's self. Jesus said, "Love your neighbor as yourself." There are a lot of people who are do-gooders and who build philosophies on doing for others. If you truly listen to them, you realize that all the do-gooding is wearing them down, leading them to be bitter and manipulative. We can only love our neighbor as we love ourselves. Only if I can take care of me can I serve you. You are working in a limited body; it only has so much energy, if you deplete your emotional energy because you have gone through a difficult day don't expect to be a star at night. Don't expect to get up the next morning and be a go-getting, inspiring, aspiring person.

Recently, in the news, one of our political figures, during a national convention, took off and got lost. He left all the politicking, left the hotel, went out to a place where there was quietness, where there was a stream, and took care of himself — a wise man.

So in terms of taking care of yourself, remember that first we are committed to Spirit, inner unification, harmony and oneness. If you are committed to that, you build energy. If you keep bringing energy back in, bringing it back in, containing yourself, staying in the Presence as much as possible by stilling the mind, (which does not mean thinking) by working with the emotional system so that it doesn't fire off all over the place, so that you are caring for the body, then you have fullness. When you have that fullness, you can give and care; you can act and do. So our relationship to ourselves is to develop that inner life energy, so that we have it available for ourselves and others.

I am at the point in my life where I am convinced that most people, who do not feel good emotionally or physically, feel that way because they are not properly restored and stored up on Spiritual energy. In most instances, there would be no conflicts if people had their own container full all the time and knew how to care for it. There would be no anger, no rage. There would be very little passion, grabbing, owning, possessing. There would be a lot of quiet people living life internally.

### *Aloneness*

If you are building a relationship with yourself, you must have developed or be developing aloneness. I cannot impress that upon you enough. You must learn to be alone.

If you don't know how to be alone, you cannot build this force. And that does not mean that you cannot have marriages and families, but you must know how to be alone with yourself.

You also must have developed slowness and slowness means moving slowly, walking slowly, and eating slowly. Then it becomes an attitude. Slowness must become a part of you.

Quietness must become a part of you. The reason that we have to develop aloneness, quietness, and slowness is because only through that quieting down can we get in touch with beliefs that we must break. You cannot hear yourself if you are going very fast; all you can hear is your relationship to the world. You cannot hear the subtle fears of being wide open. When you are quiet and slow, you hear. You cannot pray to be free of nervous energy; you have to live out watching nervous energy die, as you get slower still, quieter, and have the courage to be alone.

Remember, I am expecting that you have made a commitment to wanting to be connected, to wanting to have that feeling of the flame expanding in you, of feeling you are touching Spirit most of the time. You cannot be in touch with Spirit 100% of the time, because there is too much taken from you just by being in touch with gravity. You will always have times of restoring; Jesus did, and Buddha did.

If you want to build a relationship with your own self in the world, the commitment is to take care of yourself first. By taking care of self, you build an energy orb — a life orb —- that fills one with Spirit. You do this by developing aloneness, slowness, and quietness, whereby you contact those beliefs which are the real basis of everything you do.

### Right Eating and Body Treatment

Also related to caring for the self is caring for the body. That is your journey. I do not know what it will be for you, but I will suggest what I think it is. If you want more Spiritual energy available to you, you must give your body less material that will put stress on it.

A lot of "Spiritual" people have said, "I can put anything I want in my body, or do anything to it and it won't bother me." Such statements lack a large enough understanding. You can do a lot to your body if you want to remain relatively comfortable in the human realm. But once you have made the commitment to a Spiritual way of life, you must carefully prepare it for Spiritual Energy.

Now, once prepared and well cared for, it may be possible to do anything you like to it again. But be careful, don't try this until you have properly prepared it and understood it.

I do not think you can give the body the following stress agents and expect to live spiritually connected: drugs, tobacco, and alcohol. You cannot give it the following foods: sugar and meat. And I think, in time, probably eggs, fish, cheese, salt, and this list isn't complete. My sense is that right eating is "nuts and berries."

I heard recently that you can live on $1.00 a day for food, if you were willing to eat nuts and berries.

Finally, economically and nutritionally, it all works together: we are all going in the same direction, whether we like it or not. As you read this, take it in slowly. Read lots of material in this area, and then take the action to alter your food habits gradually.

Another part of proper treatment of the body includes exercise. This body is a vehicle that has to be treated properly, just as a machine must.

The other part of proper treatment of this body is that you must rest. My assumption is that our real capacity for work is at maximum six to ten hours. All the rest of the time, you need to be with yourself and resting.

Remember, these words are said in line with our agreed goal, to release and have Spiritual energy available. We are all afraid to rest, to sleep, because we have been taught that we are wasting time, we are not accomplishing. Take good care of yourself and you will get to God.

### *The Emotional Life*
In relation to yourself, you must gain right understanding of what your emotions are and how you want to be with them. In this limited space, I can give but one foundation for understanding and being with your emotions.

Right understanding and treatment of emotions is simple — be aware, let them be present and let them process themselves through, while standing at a point of watching.

They have a natural process and they will complete themselves of their own as long as all you do is watch. If you analyze, figure out, trace back, get overly involved, try to give them some symbolic meaning on the Spiritual quest, they will have to come around again, until you get "loose" with them.

### The Mind

In relation to yourself, it is also necessary to gain right appreciation of the mind as a tool. This has been covered in earlier sections. When an experience enters your life that triggers your emotions, the mind becomes a tool for helping to process the emotional energy.

First, the mind starts chattering, which is what it is supposed to do — the emotional energy comes in and jacks up the energy in the mind. Then, the mind begins to care for the life system. It converses, dialogues, fantasizes, imagines and regenerates other emotional energy. Let your mind do that. The key is to remain detached from what your mind is doing and don't get involved in it. Stay quiet. It will take practice and time.

If you get in there with affirmations and tell yourself to be nice, pray for someone, love them, be Godly and understanding, then you are only trying to manipulate yourself around. In the process, you are not loving yourself for your natural process, which, in almost every instance, runs its course and ends. Only if you get scared and involved will it go on and on. You know that when you go through a divorce you are going to have certain thoughts, you are going to have certain feelings; when you fall in love, you are going to have certain thoughts and feelings.

We can almost write a book saying, "this is a guaranteed process of what will happen to you." So why stop it, affirm it, try to make it better, or make it go faster? Trust yourself; trust life's process. Step back, be quiet inside, as it goes on around you. Then it will end in its right time; and the next time it will end more quickly; and then, nothing.

### RELATIONSHIP TO THE EARTH

My premise is that you have made a commitment to inner unification, harmony and oneness. On that premise, how does one relate to the earth? These next words are very important when you realize that you are unified and that you want to be committed to a sense of Oneness, you recognize that you cannot harm matter or live out of harmony with anything.

Keep those words inside you because, if you really hear them and internalize them, they will lead you to have an entirely different sense of how you want to relate to all objects and inanimate forms.

For instance, you begin to realize that the food you eat, the energy you use, the water that comes from the earth, and all animal life are natural gifts to be respected and cared for. If you get a sense of that inside you, then you cannot mistreat food; you cannot overuse energy. You begin to lose that selfish action that says, "I'll use as much as I can until it all runs out."

## *Earth*

When I was traveling through the Southwest, water was a priceless commodity, and I realized what a wonderful state California is because it provides us with water through a well-designed system.

I have become extremely sensitive about how I use water. We went through drought a couple of years ago, and when the drought was over, many of us went back to using water in the same old way. I have never gone back to using water in that old way. I am very careful, for instance, when I water the plants and water runs over into a dish, I then use that water to pass on to something else, rather than just leaving it there to evaporate in the sun.

I really understand that if I don't respect the earth and pass it on to others then I am not going to have an earth here to use anymore. I wish our political parties could realize that the issue of energy is survival, not votes, and we must have a plan to care for our earth, not vie for power.

I admit this is a young awareness in my mind, but you see, when you awaken to how much your whole life is in relationship with everything, then you cannot harm anything. You cannot misuse gasoline; you cannot misuse yourself; you cannot misuse your body.

However we move to that awareness, whether it be for economic reasons, good sense, or because there isn't enough money, we must all become aware and compassionate.

### Environment

Along with building a relationship to the earth comes developing a relationship to the environment. You begin to realize that your environment has to be an expression of and congruent with who you are. You find that you cannot live in certain kinds of houses anymore, certain kinds of communities. This does not occur because you are weak or you are a hypochondriac, but because you have become sensitive and put a new value upon yourself.

Now you will only allow yourself to be in the kind of environment that is synchronistic with your inner being. I do not know how you will create this environment for yourself.

As a part of this environmental awareness, there comes a consciousness of orderliness. And as you become more orderly and sensitive within, you cannot have as much disorder surround you. Often we say to people, keep your room clean, get orderly. We have taught people to be disciplined and do things in the "right" order. Actually, it takes a long time to allow a person to find his/her right order or to discover that they want their surroundings to be an expression of their inner self. As I looked at a house while traveling, I was aware that I would not purchase a home that had a consciousness of disorder and dirt and darkness.

Now, if one looks at that from the outside view, it could be said, "Where are your guts? Why don't you go in and clean it up? You are getting persnickety." But in another sense, this is an indication of the feeling that you do not have to live in that situation or you do not want to bring that consciousness into you.

In one home I went into, the woman had died of cancer and the man had quickly left it. You could feel that consciousness there, and at this stage of my life I did not want to go through the business, the work, or the effort of cleaning that consciousness out. I would rather wait for the right place to come along, that would feel just right.

### *Material Goods*

Another realization regarding relationship to the earth is that one begins to realize the acquisition of material things must be a statement of essentialness rather than excess. Many people have thought my saying I was going to get rid of my things was denying my talents or qualities or not being kind to myself. That is not what is happening. Rather, it is a realization that I do not need all the excess I have. As I go through my home and sort things out, I really take a look at how many times this year I have worn that red shirt, even though I love it. Well, if it hasn't been used, it is excess; it is not essential.

We live in a system that perpetuates excess and supports waste. Some political parties claim they want to create new jobs, if they get into office. If this intention comes from the point of continuing excess, then we are going backwards.

### *Ownership*

Finally, regarding relating to the earth, let's consider beliefs in ownership. I do not think I can own land; I do not think I can own a home; it doesn't belong to me. It seems to be something there for me to take care of. A home isn't something I own, it is something I am given that I pay to take care of.

If you start identifying with things in that way, then you can release possessiveness and ownership. You are also able to release hurt and harm. Then if things are stolen or lost, you are not hurt by personally identifying with them.

The other part of our relationship to the earth is letting go of the desire to have what we have not been given through work or through universal spontaneity. Let's speak to some very basic laws such as stealing. We must develop an attitude towards the earth and towards material things that we only want what comes to us through right work and/or through the Universe's spontaneous generosity.

Certainly you must know that we are raised to have so much, and we keep thinking that "so muchness" must continue. Everybody wants the qualities of bigger and bigger, more and more. That is not the attitude I want to develop. I prefer the attitude that what is mine comes to me through the Universe's willingness to give it to me, and it is there because of right action; otherwise, I do not want it in my life.

In *"The Prophet"*,[54] Gibran states:

> *Speak to us of buying and selling. And he answered and said. "To you the earth yields her fruit and you shall not want if you know how to fill your hand. It is in exchanging the gifts of the earth that you find abundance and are satisfied. Yet, unless the exchange be in love and kindly justice, it will only lead to greed and others to hunger. When in the market place you toilers of the sea and fields and vineyards meet the weavers and the potters, and the gatherers of spices, invoke then the master Spirit of the earth to come into your midst and sanctify the scales and the reckoning that weighs value against value. And suffer not the barren hand to take part in your transactions who excel their words for your labor. To such men you should say, come with us to the fields, or go with our brothers to the sea and cast your own nets. For the land and the sea are bountiful to everyone. And if there come the singers and the dancers and flute players, buy of their gifts also. For they too are gatherers of fruit and frankincense and that which they bring, the fashioned of dreams, as raiment and food for your soul. And before you leave the market place see*

---

[54] Khalil Gibran, *The Prophet,* p. 37-38.

*that no one has gone his way with empty hands.*
*For the Master Spirit of the earth shall not sleep*
*peacefully upon the wind 'til the needs of the least*
*of you are satisfied.*

### HUMAN RELATIONSHIPS

Remember, the following words are stated only because it is assumed the reader has made, or is preparing to make, a commitment to inner unification, harmony and oneness.

### Honesty with Feelings

In terms of human relationships, first we must become very honest with our feelings and judgments with regard to other people.

What am I feeling and how am I judging?

Now this is not done with a self-judgment that says there is something wrong with me or I shouldn't be judging or feeling a certain way. Instead, just allow yourself to feel those feelings and process them through.

If you are allowed to feel what you feel, you watch, you grow, and the feelings unravel themselves in their own time. However, behind this self-acceptance, I have one intention, a spiritual one, to release all biases. That is my primary goal in working with humanity, to release all biases.

### Neutrality

That does lead to a kind of neutrality, and if you aim toward no biases and neutrality, then you do not respond emotionally to much of life. You lose politicality[55]. You lose issuism. You become neutral.

Most of us are afraid to become neutral. Remember, neutral is that space of the dark night which is grey, where all beliefs are broken down.

My ideal for relating with people is that I become Love. When I was interning as a minister under Charles Roth[56], we were talking about human feelings. We had talked about all of them and finally reached love. I said to him, "What about love, Charles?"

He said, "Love is the absence of all feeling."

---

[55] [You move to a truly neutral internal place of not preferring one position over its opposite. This is true in politics (politicality) and on issues (issuism).] ed. Coy F. Cross II

[56] Charles Roth was minister of Unity Truth Center in Indianapolis, Indiana for thirty years.

I was so angry at his response that I didn't talk to him for a day, because I didn't want to hear that. I should remember my own initial response when I see others react similarly at my saying, "Loving is being neutral. Loving is not being for or against. Loving is not praying with a goal in mind. Loving is a state of being."

If you carry out this kind of loving, commit yourself to it; practice it. Once again you are releasing the belief in ownership: I can't own anyone, keep them, keep them coming to my church. I don't own any part of anyone. This attitude takes care of the law of coveting: I only have what is mine, I cannot own what belongs to anyone, nor own them.

In working with someone very close to you, again recognize your own feelings, allow them to go through and process themselves. They will, as long as you continue to prod yourself to remain detached. Once again, release your belief in ownership. Perhaps even marriage has no place in spiritual relationships. It means that one's sense about marriage and all its contingencies automatically alters. I do not know what happens externally. But there must be a deep realization that "I cannot own you."

If your life changes and wants to take you somewhere else, you must go and do that. I stand here and I watch it unfold, and as I do, I know that every action anybody takes in the Universe causes another action in me, and another in you, and another in me. Each of those will lead to right unfoldment. But I cannot hold you; I cannot keep you; I cannot own you. And that is true of children, too. We must learn to let go.

## INTIMATE RELATIONSHIPS

Intimate relationships demand that we be careful that we are with someone who is an expression of ourselves as well.

If you are living with somebody who is out of sync with who you are, you cannot hope to have your Spiritual energy available to you for any kind of ongoing unification.

Your energy will be used for handling and coping with that relationship. And if you want to make your life a life of service to handle and cope with that relationship, that is fine, do it. But know you cannot release the hidden splendor within yourself, because your emotional, mental and physical energy is being used in coping. If your emotional, mental and physical energy in bits and pieces or total amounts are being used to cope, the hidden splendor cannot be fired.

In stating that your intimate partner must be congruent with who you are, I do not mean the same as your personality, your ethics, morality, or synchronistic with your job or friends. I mean that your intimate partner must be congruent with your inner being, your soul.

You could be miles apart in terms of what you do, but be one in terms of the soul awareness. Placing your body near another for 24 hours a day demands harmony of the soul. If that harmony is missing, you will have to get free from that person in order to get on with your own path.

### *Sexuality*

I sincerely believe that the further along you move in terms of Spiritual awareness, the more you realize you do not want to dissipate your energy into sexual expression. Nor do I think anyone can do anything to make this happen before its time.

Probably all I am doing is validating those of you who have found that your sexual interest is lagging.

If this has not already happened, don't try to make it happen.

In other words, that sexual energy may be changing because of Spiritual evolution rather than the old psychological reasons, emotional reasons, because you have been damaged, or because there is something wrong with your life. You are evolving. Since the chakras move from lower to higher, it would seem to me that as you evolve, the lower chakras made whole, would gradually lose their attraction. The chakra system would evolve upward and outward as the consciousness does.

I do not think you should make this happen before it is time. When its time comes, it comes. As this evolves, the interest in sex is just not there; it is not a sickness.

Another aspect of sexuality is that we must be very careful to not allow our frustrations to come out in sexual activity. I have spent a lot of energy sexually, through frustration. I did not understand that my sexual expression, too, wanted to be/had to be synchronistic with my soul. When frustrated, I have wanted to share sexually and so I have shared sexually. When wanting something else, but not knowing how to get it, I have expressed myself sexually in order to feel as if I were in love again. When lacking in emotional fervor and questioning whether I was still in love, I have used sex to attempt to recreate that energy of passion, not knowing that I was just hooking myself again for a letdown further down the road.

I believe that sex is an expression of love and that it is an absolutely right expression of love. When the system is harmonious, it wants to move out and join with another.

If we really want to commit ourselves to the Spiritual path, this is an area where we really want to be careful. The inner prayer at this point would be that my highest desire is to express sexually from a point of love inwardly, rather than from frustration or hoping to bring the bond back again or to make up for the distance — all those good reasons that we use, which is how I think a lot of sex is expressed.

### RELATIONSHIP TO WORK

As you can see, most of these issues are parallel and overlap. Work must be congruent with one's belief. This may cause you to face yourself in a poignant area. If you are committed to Oneness, unification and harmony, then your work will have to be congruent with your beliefs. This necessarily includes the way you relate to the personnel, the atmosphere, and what is being produced.

The other attitude essential to work is that we practice the Presence as we do our work no matter what it is.

### RELATIONSHIP TO CHANGE, DEATH, LIFE

Probably the highest ideal we can have is that we become, that we let our whole doing be, the willingness to change. All I have really been sharing is that we be an ongoing vessel for change.

Mike Ivie[57] did a wonderful thing for all of us in the San Francisco area recently, when after retiring six weeks prior, he came out of retirement. When he came back he merely said, "I can change my mind."

He changed. People have looked at me all my life and said, "You changed your mind." They used to be able to catch me with that one. Now I say, "Yup, I changed my mind. Don't count on me for anything, just watch what I do. Don't even listen to my words." Right this minute you are reading my ideas, right? Well, five years ago I taught some ideas that are nearly opposite to what I teach now.

I hope that your commitment will be to allow yourself to continually die. Paul[58] said it so well, "I die daily."

I never understood when I first heard those words that they meant not just dying to the bad, which is where my mind was then, but the willingness to die to everything. Die to everything you said yesterday; die to your beliefs; to be willing to die because you know someday you are

---

[57] First baseman for the San Francisco Giants 1978-1981.

[58] Saint Paul

going to have to die. Frankly, sometimes I can't wait.

I was thinking about it today, thinking about how I was going to die. I had a wonderful fantasy, that I would have the greatest trip. This is an exciting part of our life — to die. If we can spend our lives dying each moment, then we have eternal spring and the now. If you can live in the now, fear loses its power — although it never goes away.

In bringing this material to a close, I ask you to let yourself keep dying, keep changing, and keep moving on. Khalil Gibran in *"The Prophet"* says it this way:

> *Patient, over patient, is the captain of my ship. The wind blows and restless are the sails. Even the rudder begs direction; and yet, quietly my captain awaits my silence. And these my mariners, who have heard the choir of the greater sea, they too have heard me patiently. Now they shall wait no longer. I am ready. The stream has reached the sea and once more the great Mother holds her son against her breast. Fare you well, people of Orphalese. This day has ended. It is closing upon us even as the water lily upon its own tomorrow. What was given us here on earth we shall keep, and if it doesn't suffice, then again must we come together and together stretch out our*

*hands unto the giver. Forget not that I shall come back. A little while, and my longing shall gather dust and foam for another body. A little while, a moment rest upon the wind, and another woman shall bear me. Farewell to you and the youth I have spent with you. It was but yesterday that we met in a dream. You have sung to me in my aloneness, and I of your longings have built a tower in the sky. But now our sleep has fled and our dream is over, and it is no longer dawn. The noontide is upon us and our half waking has turned to fuller day, and we must part. If in the twilight of memory we should meet once more, we shall speak again together and you shall sing to me a deeper song. And if our hands should meet in another dream we shall build another tower in the sky. So saying he made a signal to the seamen and straightway they weighed anchor and cast the ship loose from its moorings, and they moved eastward. And a cry came from the people as from a single heart, and it rose into the dusk and carried out over the sea like a great trumpeting. Only Almitra was silent, gazing after the ship until it had vanished into the mist. And when all the people were dispersed, she still stood alone upon the seawall, remembering in her heart his saying, "a little while, a moment of rest upon the wind and another woman shall bear me."* [59]

---

[59] Gibran, *The Prophet*, p. 94 - 95.

# 8: QUESTIONS AND RESPONSES

## QUESTIONS REGARDING THE SECTION ON ASPIRATION

**Question:** *Does one detach quickly, by a leap?*

**Response:** No. Many detachments have to have already taken place.

**Question:** *When one functions in this detached state of existence, do they care about anything?*

**Response:** A few years ago I was scared about that same issue. I realized that my emotional system was dying quickly, and I was afraid that I would not get up in the morning, or that I might do nothing. The last thing I could lose was caring about Carol's life.

I must have spent a year with that fear of not caring. It led me to accept and then realize that emotional caring goes but the Presence expands.

This can also make you wonder about loving others, for it creates a very impersonal love. It caused me to question intimate living relationships, because it seems that all we know right now is that the only way to keep people together is through sex and emotions.

Alice Bailey has stated this by saying, "We live from the waist down." There is nothing wrong with that, and that is the only way we know how to stay with others. We do not yet know how to be with others through the heart chakra.

However, in this detached state, caring does become impersonal even in loving, intimate relationships and as a result, relationships and caring for others become freer, less burdensome and less draining, as each one is committed only to the growth of the other.

**Question:** *Don't you become quieter and less verbal, too?*

**Response:** Yes, and let me explain how that happens.

Aspiration at its ultimate inclines towards God. It is as if there is nothing left, so you might as well "go for" God. That is an honest statement. You have done everything else by the time this movement enters your life; you have accomplished it all. The natural silence and quietness which comes is the only way to make any sense of the external world. Through the silence comes both appreciation of the Spiritual realm of life and an understanding of the intricacies of the material world.

**Question:** *Can a person have any control over this process — maybe even avoid it?*

**Response:** Let's recognize some basic factors which precede this occurrence. A person can live his entire life from a point of control. If that is the case, then he/she believes they can operate by manipulating external life. That means you believe you are in charge, your will is the operator, and, functioning with this belief, you can do a fine job.

I lived a long time like that, even though I talked about God, preached God. Then it seems I entered a time of fear, where everything said, "Nope, you are not in charge and you never were."

Remember, this is an evolutionary process. It is right for us to develop our ego and control and then it is right for such control to leave.

This leads to the question, who is in charge? Your soul is in charge — your soul always has been (even though you thought you were doing it), and it brings you all opportunities and experiences.

Once control is sent away, one learns only to watch. Now, I watch. There is a process. Spirit grows. Its time appears in the growth of body, mind, and emotions as was stated earlier.

Spirit begins to show itself after all the other work is done, and it seems to show at a point where it is essential to control. Then you must learn to smile, after you have grimaced for a long time. One goes through the experience of Job[60], a long, grey period where you can make no sense of anything. During this period you are giving up control and learning that life is not yours to control and manipulate.

Life is an experience to be lived as it comes along. This is not predestination. Predestination is explaining life at a mental level, as the only way out. This attitude towards life, a spiritual attitude, is appreciating that our souls are in charge — life is living what is. Thus, one learns to live the flow, rather than to block it off based upon one's set-

---

[60] Job from "The Book of Job in the Bible"

goals or judgments and conditionings of right and wrong.

**Question:** *Does this switch sometimes hurt physically?*

**Response:** Yes, it may hurt physically. It hurts every part of us because it is so against the way we have been prepared to live. The hurt may show as major physical disorders, neurotic tendencies, extreme anxiety, or a general malaise. By whatever name, it is the activity of Spirit, pressing in, pressing on.

**Question:** *What is the role of "the church" in this process? Why hasn't organized religion taught this extensively?*

**Response:** Clearly, aspiration is the power that motivates human beings to embark upon a spiritual path. Often, however, not trusting our own inner knowing as to how to proceed, we turn to organized religion for guidance and direction.

But what has organized religion done so often? Organized religion has consolidated the church, "monumentalized" it and turned it into something that censors the very people who created it. Organized religion has rigidified aspiration by setting down rules for how to think and act. Because of its imposed limitations, and its strict

179

regulation of ideas, organized religion too often fails us.

What about churches? Why then, do they exist? I hope your answer is that churches exist because people created them. We all built our churches. Why? Because the aspiring quality lives within us. The church is a manifestation of this human drive. It has nothing of itself to give us; we forget that. Aspiration works inside each of us, and churches merely provide us a place to pursue that together.

## *QUESTIONS REGARDING THE SECTION ON ASPECTS OF THE SPIRITUAL PATH*

**Question:** *Beingness sounds bland. Don't you miss the sunburst, the creativity?*

**Response:** In the conscious stage, you are creating, and in beingness, the exciting realization is that you are created through.

The only way I know how to answer the question about sunburst is to ask you to recognize that we have value judgments on sunbursts and the being state. All I know is that this is where "I am", and it surprises me that I don't experience ecstasy, I just experience quiet peace. It has felt a lot like boredom, and I have never denied that. What I found with boredom was that it was more fear to wear out!

I have presented a classical path. If you were to go through the Gurdgieff, Eddy, Aurobindo, Meher Baba systems[61], you would find that they say the same, but not in my words, of course.

---

[61] Georges Ivanovitch Gurdgeiff (also spelled Gurdjieff), Mary Baker Eddy, Sri Aurobindo, and Meher Baba are all spiritual thought leaders with systems.

They would say that this is how it is to be supported, this is where you are moving to, and generally this is what happens. That is my only documentation other than my own experience. I didn't set out to have this happen to me. I never would have set it up consciously, and most people who have lived it out say the same thing.

I remember one night sitting in a class and saying to a teacher who was describing how wonderful nirvana was, "That sounds boring; I don't want anything to do with it." Two years later, there I was doing boring nirvana! I didn't ask for it. I didn't want anything to do with it. The process, natural and clear because it is what it is, took me there.

**Question:** *I have experienced many dark periods; how is the dark night different?*

**Response:** Before, my dark periods had come as a result of an emotional upheaval, a physical discomfort, a difficult experience, or a reaction. But this period became a part of my life. It had nothing to do with anything else. It was a movement.

The dark night of the soul is a difficult time of groping, making one's way in the darkness.

Chardin talks about groping as an aspect of nature, science and life, as if there is a principle of the Universe, an undeniable part of life — groping. The dark night of the soul is limbo.

"Now where do you want me to put my feet? Where is the ground?"

Everybody talks these days about being grounded. Well, here there is no ground: "I am just hanging out here in the middle of nowhere, and I hate the feeling . . . so give me a body. . . ."

And the Lord says, "You can't find yourself."

There is a significant dark night of the soul. It is a vital part of life to be lived; it moves to expansion, new beingness and is usually devoid of external cause.

**Question:** *If the dark night of the soul is as you describe it, how do you get through it?*

**Response:** It is important to sit inside yourself and say, "Whatever I am being, I am being. However, you want to serve through me, serve through me. I am not attached to any way that you serve through me."

You only do what you do as you do it, and frankly, you then learn to live life now. Not a now without the past or the future, but a now incorporating all of those.

## QUESTIONS REGARDING THE SECTION ON PARTICIPATION

**Question:** *In making such changes in lifestyle and relationships, aren't there fears?*

**Response:** Yes. Such decisions and changes, of course, create fear and doubt. It is an essential period that you have to move through where you realize you cannot do what you used to do.

Then, of course, comes the threat to the relationship, the job, the threat to your own self because you were "shaped" and "formed" in another way.

It is a frightening experience to come to the awareness that you cannot do it all, and then finally realize you don't want to do it all, that you never should have done what you used to do, at all!

I understand that those of you reading this are involved in vital, well-paid jobs, important positions, families, etc. I do not know where you are going to do your job. I understand that I am a threat because I am implying that you may be forced to alter many of your present relationships to work, people, goals, etc.

My faith in you is that your process will allow you to discover the way for you to do what you seek to do.

There are lots of clever things you can do: you can find jobs where you may have to diminish the demands of your lifestyle in order to have the kind of expression that allows you to financially provide for your needs. You do have to give up a lot. Usually it is worldly goods and money for a while.

When I signed the final papers on my house, in 1980, I realized the profit was less than I thought it was going to be. Then the thought came to me that it is only going to be what it is going to be. Then I decided to pay off my car and I looked at the expenses I was to have starting September 1, 1980. There was to be a $100 interest check, food and low rent, approximately $300 total. Before the house was sold, my expenses were between $900 and $1100 a month. As I wrote my bills it was uncanny to realize that I had just cut my expenses from $1100 a month to $300 a month.

There is a way for you to do it; no matter how many bills you have, you are not stuck. No matter how many children you have, you are not stuck, you are not stifled.

**Question:** *Isn't it the ego which keeps us from taking such risks?*

**Response:** Yes, the belief is really the ego, but I think it is more fair to say that a lot of it is the actual living out. If somebody reading this has four children and a husband/wife, and is working to help pay for the house they never could afford in this area, to say that it is just ego is unkind. It is so much more: it is all the responsibilities that gradually have to be seen through and released step-by-step and over a period of time.

**Question:** *This sounds like a narcissistic, ingrown process and dangerous! It even sounds like a denial of your talents, potential, gifts, and society.*

**Response:** All I can say is that I do not feel "denial," and I do not feel I am ignoring my talents. In fact, one of my greatest hang-ups has been that I am so talented that I have felt it essential to express them all. I no longer feel driven to express them all. I want to express one, which is that ongoing feeling of connection with the Spirit within. I believe that I am going to find a way to feel that within myself so completely that talent, potential and activity in society will be expressed through me in a new way.

I have done a lot of letting go prior to taking the action of changing my lifestyle, diminishing my goods and aiming towards a quiet, private life, or I never could have made such a sharp break with my heritage and lifestyle. The ego belief was a powerful thing for me to cope with, but finding a way to work it out took a much longer time in the practical, everyday world.

**Question:** *When you experience this energy, it is like my experience as an artist. I'll be sitting, working, and all of a sudden a high-speed energy hits me, frightens me. I get up and walk around my chair just to try to handle it. If that is the case, how do you handle it?*

**Response:** First, yes, it sounds like the same. How do you handle it? How you described yourself is how I was today when I went into the store. I felt so wide open, so high, transcendent, expanded out beyond myself. Being in that place I felt that I had to get home, to ground myself. That is one of the things we must do to handle this, ground ourselves.

I do believe that the more we adjust to it, the more willing each of us will be to be in that space for periods of time.

Also, remember that when it enters and it has gone by, you feel a definite pull down, not a let-down, but a pull-down. It's as if your body has had so much channeled through it that the body tires and has to rest, be flattened, until its batteries are restored to channel again.

For years, people have said that when one gets spiritual, they will be able to take "IT" all. No, the body must be developed in order to handle "IT" all, and all of the systems must be developed enough to understand "IT". IT, literally, is like having a huge blast of electrical power go through all your systems and they can get blown out!

**Question:** *Do you believe there is more of this energy around now and with this available, can we, should we, protect ourselves?*

**Response:** There does seem to be more of it around. If you do feel a lot of high energy, what I often do is to NOT let myself receive all of it. Such action tends to thrust the energy into the top of my head. If I let that happen, then I have a longer period of adjustment. I cover it up, put a lid on it — it is a pretending, but it works! If so much is going through you that you feel like you are leaving your body, then you cannot relate to life, to anything; nor can you function. That is not right for me. In fact, a lot of these spiritual experiences have psychological terminology to them that sounds like craziness.

If you are interested and/or concerned about these similarities, you should read some of the articles and books which address the subtleties, such as the back section of "*Stalking The Wild*

*Pendulum"* by Bentov, *"The Kundalini Experience: Psychosis or Transcendence"* by Lee Sinella, and *"Kundalini"* by Gopi Krishna.

This experience often is called "the awakening of the Kundalini," which means that all the chakras are hooked up, aligned, and a tremendous serpentine energy is released which goes out through the top of the head.

When I started having these experiences, I started drawing on pads of paper a series of lines. I thought they were a symbol for being in love, but three and one half years later, at a program called, "The Spiritual Path, Pitfalls and Promises," I found it to be the serpentine symbol for Kundalini energy and infinity. The symbol was drawn through all my works for about eight months, and I thought at the time that it was craziness. I felt so dark and yet I was probably never more powerful, but I did not know what to do with it because I lacked understanding.

**Question:** *How do you know whether such experiences are craziness or spiritual?*

**Response:** I don't. I only know that it is a very individual experience. I know that you can create it consciously. I also know that it was not the result of negative material going on in my life. I know that the effects all have psychological labels and one of the greatest beliefs you have to break through is labeling.

You keep hearing inside, "I must be manic depressive. What's wrong with me? I've never been emotionally out of order before; what is wrong with me — why can't I control this?" And then one day, you just quit and let it be what it will be.

**Question:** *Do you ever feel just plain flat?*

**Response:** Oh, yes and flat is horrible for me. When that precious energy, that connection is not there, it is horrible. To me, flatness is the dark night of the soul. I don't know depression anymore. I haven't had a depressed day since August of 1977. I don't know depression but I know flatness. I also don't know emotional highs anymore. But I do know transcendence.

People who know me intimately comment that the change in my personality is remarkable; before they experienced me as a roller coaster. I still feel like I have this expansion and then this flat space, but my being, the inner "I" remains stable. Carol Knox has become a stable human being.

**Question:** *In your description, you mentioned no excitement, flatness, etc. That sounds awful!*

**Response:** I know and I understand, and spiritual leaders will all tell you that one of the hardest things to give up is the high, the pleasure.

I do not experience pleasure or excitement in the ways I did before. It really hurt as it changed. I was no longer inclined in ways I used to be. That shift was brutal.

It takes brutal honesty to become so self-aware, and only as you quiet the mind can you have that kind of honesty.

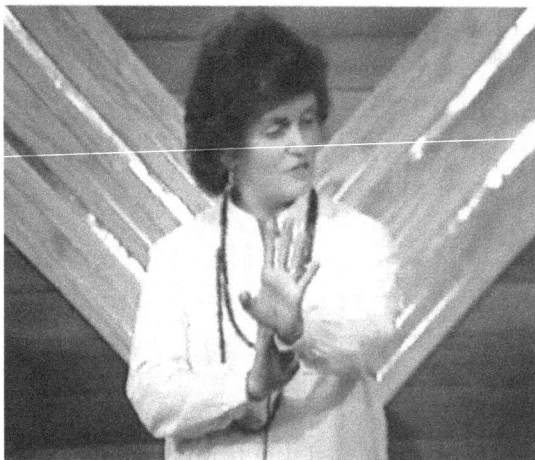

Here is a warming thought: I experience what can only be called spiritual joy. It is not the joy that is opposite to sorrow, it is another joy — deeper, ongoing, always. Presence!

## QUESTIONS REGARDING THE SECTION ON DEVELOPING CONSCIOUSNESS

**Question:** *Instead of going through all the discomfort, why not just get centered, be still, go to the center in the eye of the hurricane? Why does there have to be so much discomfort and pain and struggle?*

**Response:** In order to reach the eye of the hurricane you must walk through from the outer circumference into the center. That is walking through the fire, going through body, mind, emotions, and environment to get to the center.

You see, if you leap, then you don't live it out and discover that God is everywhere — in the circumference and in the center! Not until you realize that can you stand in the center. You have to go through it all to get there. There is no other way through.

And when you get to the center, you have a jewel of great price, for you experience love in the midst of all.

Also you realize the center is the whole, the whole is the center — indeed, there is no center, it is all the center. There is nowhere to get to or go to once you fully realize and internalize this. All is holy.

**Question:** *Why do people find it so hard to love God? And what does it mean to love God?*

**Response:** I have wondered about that, too, for I wanted to love God but couldn't do it easily at all. I guess the present, clearest answer for me is that people hate to be second. Loving God means that God becomes first. It means a way of life, an attitude, a commitment to let God be first. It is an inspired way of living, isn't it? It touches you, doesn't it? And in that we get a glimmer of why loving God is so powerful!

Not wanting God, or not wanting to keep your mind on God, is not at all uncommon.

The early church fathers wrote about their dry, dusty, difficult times with it. Theophan the Recluse states, "There must needs be patience, labor, and sweat for the attention runs away." You see, your attention always wants to run away from God, even if you make the commitment.

Please realize that it doesn't automatically just attend to God because you say so! My inner prayer often would be "Please let me love you; help me to want to do this thing I have to do; I don't want to love you, God. I want to stay out there and play."

I have no recourse now, but at the same time, I have practiced for a number of years!

Yes, the attention runs away, the heart feels nothing — flat. It has no desire to pray. That is one of the most difficult aspects of this first stage of prayer of the heart feels nothing. You listen to someone like me say there is so much joy to all this, and then you start practicing, saying, "Oh, Jesus Christ, have mercy." And in the back of your mind you are saying, "Oh, for God's sake, this is the stupidest thing I've ever done in my life. How did I ever get into this? I feel dry, dusty, dirty, in the middle of a desert and there's no water. I can't feel anything singing in my heart yet." And a year later you are still doing it. "Where's that feeling? At least with the other life there were ups and downs."

This desire to love God and the actual loving of God is tough! Yet, there are no greater, more haunting love songs for anybody than there are for God.

Theophan the Recluse states, "Yet in spite of this, give yourself a moderate rule and keep to it. Be outer in reading, inner in thoughts of God. Outer in love of wisdom, inner in love of God. Outer in words, inner in prayer. Outer in technique, inner in vision."

## QUESTIONS REGARDING THE SECTION ON PHILOSOPHY OF LIVING/DOING THE SPIRITUAL LIFE

**Question:** *It is uncomfortable living this way, isn't it?*

**Response:** Well, there are two states of

discomfort, external discomfort and becoming comfortable with the discomfort. If you feel you are right in being at the place of discomfort, then you understand that is where you are to be. If you realize that something needs to be understood in order to move you to the next space, you may be taken out of that place of discomfort.

Let me state this again. It is very important! You have a sense that it is right for you to be in a place that is not comfortable; you know wherever you are, you are to be; you understand that you are at that place as a place for clarification and refinement, to lead you to the next place.

**Question:** *But isn't the goal to be comfortable?*

**Response:** Yes. But something important must be said here too: the intention is not just to become comfortable; the intention is to be at peace with wherever you are — even peaceful with being uncomfortable!

Remember, the "way" to become comfortable is through active participation as presented in the third chapter.

*Question: Living like this sounds as if order and discipline no longer apply.*

**Response:** "Order" and "discipline" are words to which we give special power as though it were possible to impose a discipline and an order from outside ourselves. True order comes from within.

If only we all had a way to live on this planet so that we did not have to show up at work at a certain time. If only we had a way to break the fear that we would do nothing if our disciplines and order were taken away from us.

One of my greatest fears has been that if I allow myself to be this free, to move this much in the flow of my being, that having no "responsibility," I might become depressed — I might lie down and die.

You see, it is so much a part of us, to have an imposed order and discipline. But, if you could break through those fears, you would find out that there is an absolute inner order. There is a time to get up and a time to go to sleep; a time to do your project, and to create the space to do that project, and a time for the project to be finished. (That does not mean completely finished — projects do not finish — life does not finish, everything keeps going on.) There is a time for everything and your inner system knows, and the inner system is the Law of Your Being.

However, our society, our limitations, and our surroundings, do not allow for that. That is why I think there are going to be more and more people who are going to say, "I have to find another way to live."

People like you are going to have to say that. You will not be psychotic in realizing this; you will be very clear. The more people that realize this, the sooner we will form new ways of coping with our present issues.

This brings me again to the statement I made earlier, that people who are willing to live from within can be frightening to others and to society in general. People who live from within may not follow social order; they may not work for a living

— they live to work; they probably do not pay insurance; they probably do not own excessive material goods which limit their mobility; they probably do not own land; they probably do not own each other; they probably do not have formal marriage relationships.

These are outrageous, frightening statements. If not understood in this context, they might be interpreted as revolutionary. But they are not. These are statements about people who know they are unfolding beings.

For example, there is no way they can remain connected with one person for any longer than the Law of Their Being intends for them to be there, nor with a job, a place or a way of expressing. This is the reason they may be disliked and called revolutionaries.

201

## QUESTIONS REGARDING THE SECTION ON RELATIONSHIPS

**Question:** *The poem by Gibran speaks to competition and non-competition. Where does competition fit in all of this?*

**Response:** I think competition is absurd, and I do it. Every time I do it, I watch and I notice. I notice especially that if somebody says, "I did this," and I respond with, "I did this," then I am aware that I am being competitive. Usually, I will stop and say, "This gets me nowhere; this isn't what is really going on in me. Something else is going on." Usually, I know what is going on beneath, and once I see it, then another old belief has lost its energy in me.

Competition is absurd; it's there for all of us, and as we watch and have courage and trust, it dies from lack of involvement and energy.

**Question:** *When you talk about right environment, what happens when what fits you does not fit your pocketbook?*

**Response:** First, I continue to be clear in terms of what fits with me — that does not go away.

What is difficult is whether my means, my emotions and my mind can allow me to always have what fits with me. I may be able to say, "I know this doesn't fit. Internally I do know, but whether I can work that out in the world, is the next question.

There are a million different facets that I do not have control over. And then I may have to be in an uncomfortable situation and be at peace with that. Everything unfolds and clarifies in order. As long as you are in the material world you will have things that you will be working with, to understand, to clarify.

## QUESTIONS REGARDING THE SECTION ON SEXUALITY

**Question:** *How would you find true sexual expression?*

**Response:** I don't know; I think it would be a good experience to find out how often the sexual desire really comes from a space of love. I am saying that the most important thing is to allow yourself to express sexually according to the way that is moving in you now — to watch and notice how often it comes from love and to make a commitment to aim toward only expressing it when it comes from love rather than frustration or trying to heal a relationship.

**Question:** *How would you know love?*

**Response:** I am sure that if it comes from love it comes from a feeling of fullness, from a giving of abundance, from a feeling of overflow. It just is there, now.

**Question:** *But didn't you say that love is the absence of feeling?*

**Response:** Yes. But the absence of feeling, the state of neutrality, does not mean death, nothingness, absence itself; only the absence of feeling as an attachment.

It is important to say that neutrality does not mean the absence of energy or the absence of a feeling of abundance, bliss, peace. It means that there is no feeling on either side of the mid-zone. The feeling of love would be to be in the middle, to be neutral, and that feeling is one of fullness and abundance.

Nobody has that feeling if they are just "playing around." There is a difference, too, in neutrality as I am explaining it and not caring and then expressing yourself with anybody sexually. These are two different stages of expression and development miles apart.

**Question:** *Is this way of expressing sexually a goal? If so, I don't like it or want it!*

**Response:** I really understand. It is not a goal. It is something that gradually happens as you evolve. I would invite you to be with this in the same way I have explained being with the emotions, the mind. Watch and notice where the sexual movement comes from and let your commitment be to expressing sexuality from a place of love. And even the concept of love will evolve.

**Question:** *Neutrality sounds scary, boring, strange.*

**Response:** It is strange, and it is one of the most frightening phases to live out. Neutrality and the fear that comes with it give the inner feeling that I might never do anything again. That fear still hits me.

Yet, amazingly, in neutrality is the purest activity. Believe it or not, we can live on this earth and move and do and give and share and perform and create and accomplish without impetus and without goals and without desire, and even without inspiration.

"In the beginning God created the heaven and the earth. And the earth was without form and void..."

It was without form and void in that presence of light. We have been afraid to be without form and void. I have been very frightened by it; but I have come to accept it and keep moving on.

*Question: Is this unconditional love?*

**Response:** Unconditional would seem to be a stage just prior to neutrality. I have not really explored unconditional love extensively. But it would seem to me, you could have unconditional love but still have some kind of emotional content in other areas.

**Question:** *When you describe nothingness, neutrality, what does it feel like; how do you get through it?*

**Response:** First, it is a big nothing and it is terrible, and you do get depressed. You don't want to live. And then forty days later, which metaphysically is the length of time it takes to complete anything, you find you are still around so you might as well get up and do something, and then you have "gotten" over the fear you might never do anything again.

The most difficult fear is that you won't move. I think you have to live that out.

There is no way for anybody to make that better except to trust. Trust!

We are all so afraid to be depressed. But depression is only being afraid to be where you are, and remember the definition of "perfect" is "as you are"!

The point is to be in the moment as it is now, and that is a definition of perfect. So you might as well be glad you are where you don't want to be — where you are is.

*Reverend Carol Ruth Knox (1986)*

# CAROL RUTH KNOX BIOGRAPHY

Carol Ruth Knox was born in Somerville, Massachusetts, near Boston, on December 16, 1938. She graduated cum laude from Tufts University in Medford, Massachusetts, receiving a Bachelor of Arts degree in Music and in English. She completed a Master of Arts degree in Musicology from Brown University in Providence, Rhode Island. Carol Ruth's doctoral degree was awarded by the California Institute of Integral Studies — San Francisco. Her dissertation explored the Prayer of the Heart, an ancient form of Christian meditation.

Prior to entering the Unity ministry, Carol Ruth taught English and Music and was Director of Music at a high school in Connecticut. She was also a Director of the Massachusetts Association for the Adult Blind.

Between 1955 and 1968 Carol Ruth toured the eastern United States as a professional concert pianist.

As a lifetime student of Unity, she completed her first Unity class in Cambridge, Massachusetts, under the guidance of the Reverend Edna Titus. She attended Unity School for Religious Studies, Unity Village, Missouri from 1968 to 1970, and was ordained as a Unity minister on Aug. 14, 1970 by the Association of Unity Churches.

Carol Ruth became minister of the Unity Center of Walnut Creek in California soon after her ordination. Taking a small group, she developed it into one of the largest ministries west of the Mississippi with nearly 400 active members. She served as the Center's minister until her death nearly seventeen years later.

Reverend Knox authored many Unity publications, lectured widely on the West Coast of the USA to professional and service clubs, conducted seminars, appeared on weekly television and radio series, and wrote a newspaper column. She conducted workshops and taught classes throughout Unity and was also deeply engaged in the greater community thereby making a positive impact in the world.

On February 1, 1987, Reverend Carol Ruth Knox was killed by an intruder in her home in Antioch, California, thus ending the life of a visionary and living example of God's Love. Her legacy of passion, wisdom, and faith continues to change the lives of everyone who reads or hears her words.

# ENGAGE WITH COY F. CROSS II:

## ON FACEBOOK

https://www.facebook.com/CoyFCrossIIPhd

## ON YOUTUBE

http://www.youtube.com/channel/UCfb8JPMD9P4
6pQHLmE1uN0Q

## ON TWITTER

https://twitter.com/coy_ii

## ON THE WEB

Search "Coy F Cross" for interviews and more. You can also visit http://thedhance.com to enjoy more of Coy.

# CAROL RUTH KNOX PRESENTED BY COY F. CROSS II

For more information about Carol Ruth Knox and her pioneering spiritual work visit: the website http://CarolRuthKnox.com *(directly below)*.

Or you can find her work on Facebook *(directly below)*.

https://www.facebook.com/revcarolruthknoxphd

# COY CROSS II IN PERSON

For more information about Coy F. Cross II and his transformational workshops go to either of his websites:

- Being Fully Present in Caregiving
- Dealing with Crisis in Caregiving
- Practical Spirituality
- The Dhance
- The Path of Acceptance
- The Gift of Acceptance
- and more ...

The Dhance Events          Carol Ruth Knox Events

# COY CROSS II IN PRINT

## The Dhance: A Caregiver's Search for Meaning

*The Dhance: A Caregiver's Search for Meaning by Coy F. Cross II, Ph.D.* - Practical Spiritual Help for a Crisis - Buy it now at http://TheDhance.com

*A Message from Coy F. Cross II, Author, about The Dhance* - In 2009, my precious wife, Carol Martha, and I were told she had Stage 3, Level C ovarian cancer. We were thrown into confusion and fear, but quickly decided to use the training we had been given years ago by Reverend Carol Ruth Knox. This wasn't the path I'd expect on my way to God, but this is the path I've been given. These past three years [2009-2012] have been my 'graduate course' in deepening my relationship with the Divine. I have experienced a curious mixture of great pain and great joy. I have seen God in the faces of doctors, nurses, cancer patients and grieving families. There has been an abundance of loving kindness from perfect strangers. Finally, I have loved and been loved more deeply than I could ever imagine. I have come to know that God is right here, right now, in the midst of this terrible disease called cancer.

But my search isn't over and I don't expect it to reach its end until my end. "Wherever I am, God is, and all is well."

Testimonials

Coy F. Cross II PhD

**The Path of God**

Coy F. Cross II has also edited a book of Carol Ruth Knox's talks called, *The Path of God*.

Reverend Knox was one of the front-runners in New Age spiritual thinking. The chapters in this book are a series of talks that she gave sequentially at Unity of Walnut Creek from January to March 1986.

Reverend Carol Ruth Knox built Unity of Walnut Creek from a 20-person-Sunday-morning congregation into a center of three Sunday services with 450 people attending. Her secret: she saw God in flowers and trees, in dogs and birds, in the desert and the ocean, and in the affluent and the indigent. God included every-thing both the animate and inanimate. And everything in God's Creation created an opportunity for spiritual growth.

Each Sunday she shared how she had encountered God in the past week and the lessons she had learned. Reverend Knox challenged her audience with quantum physics, philosophy, Eastern Religions, and whatever subject that caught her interest.

She possessed the unique gift of being able to explain the most complex ideas so that people could understand; and, she expected her congregation to be sophisticated and to accept responsibility to understand. She never 'talked down' to those attending her church. As a result, each Sunday attendees would leave with tools to help them in their daily lives.

Tragically in 1987, Carol Ruth Knox was murdered by an intruder in her home. But her powerful and truly relevant messages still resonate today and can help one achieve a life of meaning, of service and of spiritual mastery by embracing The Path of God.

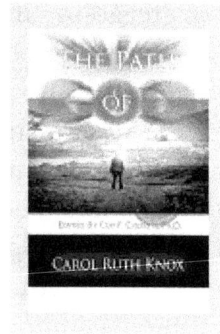

## Other books by Coy F. Cross II include:

- _Lincoln's Man in Liverpool: Consul Dudley and the Legal Battle to Stop Confederate Warships_ (2007),
- _Justin Smith Morrill Father of the Land-Grant Colleges_ (1999),
- _From the Stone Age to the Space Age: a History of Beale AFB_ (1997),

- *Go West Young Man! Horace Greeley's Vision for America* (1995),

Coy F. Cross II has jointly authored the following Monograph with Roger D. Launius:

- *MAC and the Legacy of the Berlin Airlift* (Monograph of the Military Airlift Command, Office of History) (1989).

# Unity of Walnut Creek

- A supportive spiritual community
- Prayer support
- Spiritual growth
- Classes and workshops
- Making a difference

There is also a detailed history of Reverend Carol Ruth Knox at Unity of Walnut Creek: on the website as well as a historical timeline.

http://www.unityofwalnutcreek.com/

www.ingramcontent.com/pod-product-compliance
Lightning Source LLC
Chambersburg PA
CBHW071335090426
42738CB00012B/2903